CHOICES THAT MAKE OR BREAK

LIFEWORK PRESS

CHOICES THAT MAKE OR BREAK

People in the Bible, the Choices They Made, Factors that Drove those Choices, and How their Choices Impacted their Lives and Legacy.

GLORIA GODSON

LIFEWORK PRESS

CHOICES THAT MAKE OR BREAK VOLUME 1

LifeWork Ministries, Inc.
 P. O. Box 56
Townsend, DE 19734
www.lifeworkministries.org
lifeworkministriesinc@gmail.com

Lifework Press ©

2022 by Gloria Godson

All rights reserved solely by the author. No part of this book may be reproduced in any form without the permission of the author. For permission requests, contact author at www.lifeworkministries.org.

Unless otherwise indicated, Scripture quotations taken from the Holy Bible, New Living Translation (NLT). Copyright ©1996, 2004, 2007 by Tyndale House Foundation. Used by permission of Tyndale House Publishers, Inc.

Scripture quotations taken from the New King James Version (NKJV)–*public domain*.

Printed in the United States of America.

ISBN: 978-81-951122-0-3

Dedicated

to

my Friend and Partner, Holy Spirit,

my trusted guide in decision making

And

The Word of the Living God, a Lamp to

My Feet and a Light to my path

CONTENTS

Introduction

Chapter 1—The People's Man..................................1

Chapter 2— Middle East Greed............................18

Chapter 3—Behold El Roi.......................................74

Chapter 4—The High Cost of Low Living...................96

Afterword 129

INTRODUCTION

Choices of the heart is a 1983 movie about the life of Jean Donovan, a beautiful young woman who went from being a free spirited college student, to a deeply committed missionary. Jean gave up her family, friends, and finances and moved to El Salvador to work among the poor. In her letters to her family back in the U.S, Jean said over and over again, that God brought her to El Salvador. Unfortunately, in December 1980, she and three nuns were tortured and killed by members of the El Salvador national guard.

Jean's story sounds like a modern-day rendition of the stories of Stephen, apostle Paul, apostle James, apostle Peter, and so many others, whose choices to follow Jesus Christ cost them their lives. Today, around the world, more than three hundred and forty million Christians live in places where they experience high levels of persecution, just for following Christ. Here in America, Christians are increasingly coming under intense persecution for their faith.

The question is, what is the right response to these challenges? Should Christians cower in fear, back down, and try to appease their persecutors, or should they be bold and courageous in their witness for Christ? The answer is deeply personal, but it all comes down to choices. The ordinary choices we make each day, will determine the outcome of the rest of our lives.

This book examines the lives of people in the Bible, the choices they made, the factors that drove those choices, the outcomes they experienced, and how their choices had a profound impact on their lives and legacy. First Corinthians 10:6-11 states that these real life Bible accounts are recorded as examples for us, to help us to make the right choices for our lives. The things that happened to these people are written down as a warning to us, so that we would not make the same mistakes that they made. This is because, wrong choices with tragic consequences don't often appear huge at the time. They may be "little" things like wanting something so much that we are willing to compromise biblical principles to get them, or grumbling and complaining about life circumstances.

This book addresses these and other critical issues of life and legacy. Our daily choices can make or break us. For Jean, her choice to serve God in El Salvador led to her death. One might reason that if she did not answer the call of God on her life, and chose instead to remain in America, she might have lived a much longer life. But we would probably not be talking about her today. She would most likely have lived a relatively more comfortable life, but the impact of her life and legacy would be vastly different.

I pray that this book will help us to learn from the lives of the people who have gone before us, so that we will determine to live our lives by God's design, experience God's best in every area of our lives, and leave a legacy of faith that will inspire future generations.

CHAPTER 1
THE PEOPLE'S MAN

AARON

Aaron was the brother of Moses and the first high priest of Israel. We are first introduced to him in Exodus 4. This is when God called Moses at the burning bush and told him to go back to Egypt and lead the Israelites out of bondage. Moses protested and told God that He had the wrong guy. He insisted that he was not qualified for the job because he had a speech impediment, and asked God to send someone else. Then God said to Moses: "All right, what about your brother Aaron, the Levite? I know he speaks well. He will be your spokesman." So, Aaron was appointed by God Himself to be Moses' right hand man in the important work of birthing a nation.

I am thankful that the Bible recorded the dialogue between Moses and God. It is a great blessing to me, because I often feel like

Moses, totally unqualified! It is truly amazing the types of people God chooses to do His work. Rarely does God tap a person on the shoulder for an assignment, and they think, "Of course, I am the logical pick!" When God called Gideon to go and fight the fearsome Midianites, he was in hiding, threshing wheat in a wine press. God uses the most unlikely people. Someone has said that "God doesn't call the qualified, He qualifies the called." In 1 Corinthians 1: 26-29, apostle Paul agrees. He explains "Brothers and sisters, consider your calling: Not many were wise from a human perspective, not many powerful, not many of noble birth. Instead, God has chosen what is foolish in the world to shame the wise, and God has chosen what is weak in the world to shame the strong. God has chosen what is insignificant and despised in the world, what is viewed as nothing, to bring to nothing what is viewed as something, so that no one may boast in His presence." So, if you are feeling totally unqualified for God's call on your life, you are in good company. Chuck Swindoll has said, "You may feel unqualified, uneducated, untrained, under-gifted or even unworthy, yet... those are excellent qualifications for God to do a mighty work.

Moses felt very unqualified, but with God's promise and Aaron as his spokesman, he agreed to go back to Egypt. Aaron met him in the wilderness, and together, they returned to Egypt and worked as a team to bring the children of Israel out of bondage. After they left Egypt, Moses and Aaron navigated tremendous challenges as they brought the Israelite multitude through the wilderness. But, they also experienced tremendous victories! Together they saw, first-hand, the miraculous hand of God in His judgement of the ten plagues in Egypt. They watched Him drown Pharaoh and his army in the red sea. They saw God provide, again and again, for His people in the wilderness, and Aaron was there when the Lord gave Israel the ten commandments on mount Sinai. He worked with Moses to build the wilderness tabernacle, and in Exodus 29, Aaron and his sons were, by God's command, consecrated to the Lord as priests.

The role of a priest is to represent God to the people and to represent the people to God. A priest was a mediator between God and man, and the priesthood was a high and holy office. Aaron had clearly risen in significance and leadership among the people. He was the second in command, and was seen as God's representative and mouthpiece. People looked up to him, and he did exceptionally well when Moses was around to tell him what to do.

Then we come to Exodus 32. Moses had gone up to the mountain to meet with God, and left Aaron in charge of the camp. I imagine that Moses was confident that Aaron had matured as a leader, and was able and ready to take charge, and lead the people in his absence. Which is why what actually happened is so shocking! Exodus 32:1 states that, "When the people saw how long it was taking Moses to come back down the mountain, they gathered around Aaron. "Come on," they said, "make us some gods who can lead us. We don't know what happened to this fellow Moses, who brought us here from the land of Egypt."

Decision Drivers

There are two important factors at play here. First, Moses stayed up on the mountain longer than the people expected; and secondly, there was such a large leadership vacuum in Moses's absence, that the people came to Aaron and asked him to make them gods who can lead them. The question is, "If Moses had been there, would the people have asked for pagan gods to be made for them to lead them?" I think the answer is clearly "No", then the second question is, "Why is it that Moses' absence left such a big gap in leadership?" The answer is in the person Moses left in charge, Aaron. Moses probably thought that a man like Aaron who had worked with him side by side through the long and tedious negotiations with Pharaoh, a man like Aaron who had been the mouthpiece of God, a man who had seen first-hand God's miracles in Egypt, His mighty victory over Pharaoh at the red sea, and His miraculous provisions in the desert, a man whom God Himself selected and anointed as the first high priest of Israel, that such a man was fit to take charge and lead the people aright in his absence. But alas, Aaron was not up to the task. He was not a strong leader. In fact, there is such a lack of leadership in the camp that the people came to Aaron in search of leadership, and when he didn't provide it, they asked him to make them some gods who can lead them.

Why was it that Aaron did so well when he had Moses to tell him what to do, but crashed and burned on his very first solo flight? It appears that, unlike Moses, he did not have a personal, intimate, relationship with God that molded his character and commanded his devotion. Aaron served God as priest, but did not know God intimately, at least, not enough to know His ways and to seek to please Him alone. He served God faithfully when someone told him what to do, but did not have independent initiative or a strong and fully committed will. Aaron was a people pleaser.

Also, Aaron and the people had elevated Moses unduly and put him on a pedestal. Moses was a great leader, but he was not their god. He did not bring them out of Egypt. He was merely the leader that God used. Jehovah was their God. But they had put Moses on such a pedestal that when he was gone, they lost their spiritual moorings and drifted off to sea. This is the danger of hero-worship. When God uses someone to help us out of a very difficult situation, if we are not careful, we can knowingly or unknowingly attribute to that person, the honor, following, deference, and adoration that is due to God alone. Whether it's a pastor, gifted speaker, charismatic leader, TV preacher or healing evangelist, no human being is worthy of our worship. And when we give people undue place and elevation in our lives, it is idol worship, and that will diminish our focus on God, warp our perspective, and lead to major problems.

Additionally, Aaron felt inadequate as a leader. He did not have the great face to face encounters with God that Moses had. So, he was intimidated, discounted his own direct access to God, and instead, leaned on Moses. Up until this time, he had led in the shadow of Moses. So, when Moses was not there, his inadequacies and insecurities came to the surface. He needed the people to like him and accept him as a leader in his own right; and felt that the easiest way to achieve that goal is to give the people what they want. He did not have Moses' authentic personal authority that came from a deep relationship with God, so he opted for cheap popularity as a substitute. Aaron's failure to take his self-doubt, diffidence, and lack of confidence to God and receive divine affirmation, left him wide open for the devil's attack. When the spiritual covering of Moses was removed, Aaron's deficiency was exposed for all to see.

Aaron's Options

When the people came to Aaron and said, "make us some gods," Aaron didn't miss a beat. He didn't say, "wait a minute, let's think this through." He didn't try to stop them. Right away, he said, "Take the gold rings from the ears of your wives and sons and daughters, and bring them to me", and all the people took the gold rings from their ears and brought them to Aaron. Then Aaron took the gold, melted it down, and molded it into the shape of a calf.

Wow! This is unbelievable! Moses left Aaron in charge, but Aaron is not man enough for the job! Instead of stepping up as a leader to speak to the people, inspire them, provide godly direction, and turn them away from their idolatrous proposal, he gave them a plan and blueprint to execute it. It is sad enough that God's people would conceive this heathen proposal, after all that He had done for them. But what was most disheartening is that Aaron, God's high priest, did not oppose or object at all. He was ready, willing, and prepared, at the people's say so, to switch out his high and holy priestly garments, for the garb and tools of a pagan priest. He led God's people to reject God, and choose idols they made with their own hands. It is also surprising that Aaron knew exactly how to make the golden calf. He did not hesitate one bit! It looks like he had prior experience in this sort of thing, as if he had done this before.

Now, it's not like Aaron was out of options. Let's explore some of the other options that were available to him. He could have:

1. Focused the people on God. As God's priest, it is his job to represent God to the people.

2. Led the people into a time of prayer to seek God's presence and guidance.

3. Encouraged the people to hang in there and wait a little longer for Moses to come down.

4. Prayed to God about the situation and asked God for his direction and intervention.

5. Reminded the people of all that God had done for them in Egypt and in the wilderness.

6. Reminded them of the covenant they made with God on mount Sinai. The very first commandment is, "You shall not have any other gods beside me."

7. Aaron could have showed them how their proposal violated God's word and lead them to repentance.

These same options are open to you and I as well. When the devil tries to get you to step outside of God's word and will, when waiting becomes hard, and your soul is weary, you can encourage yourself in the Lord like David did. You can pray and talk to God about the situation, and Philippians 4:6 says that when you pray, God's peace will guard your heart; you can remind yourself of all that God has already done in your life; you can get back into the word of God and renew your mind; and you can remember the new covenant that Jesus purchased for you on the cross. Romans 8:32 says that if God freely gave you His Son, the best that heaven has, He certainly would not withhold from you anything else that He has to give.

The Timing Tension

Prolonged timing and waiting are major human weaknesses and tension points that often cause a stress fracture in the lives and faith of many Christians. What happened to the Israelites can happen to all of us. When things take longer than we expect, or when we are disappointed by outcomes that we did not expect, the devil tries to get us to vote God out of office and make ourselves new gods. He invites us to initiate a Do It Yourself (DIY) project.

This is what happened in the lives of Abram and Sarai. After ten years of waiting for the son promised by God, they were baited by the enemy into birthing an Ishmael. Ishmael was the result of their attempt to obtain the promise of God by their own self-effort. They got weary of waiting for God's timing and the devil was delighted to help them find a way to get God's promised blessing without God.

What about you, are you waiting on the manifestation of God's promise in your life? Are you weary from years of praying, weeping, and waiting for God? Now the devil is talking to you, pushing you to make your own god. He is pushing you to abandon your biblical convictions and godly principles and make a god in your own image. A god that will let you do what you want with no consequences at all. A god that will bless you on your own time table.

Sadly, so many Christians have fallen for the devil's lie. They have made gods in their own image. They have their own god, their own truth and their own morality. They have a god who "understands" their reality, who will tell them what they want to hear, and let them live the way they want to live. But that is not the God of the Bible. Their god is a make believe god, a figment of their imagination.

Unfortunately, many of these people will find out, too late, after they leave this life, that the gods they worshiped, the gods of popularity, human approval, relevance, tolerance, money, pleasure, science, and excess are not gods at all. They are merely golden calves that they had made for themselves.

The critical unanswered question is, "How can a god you made lead you?" Isaiah 44 outlines the absurdity and utter foolishness of making your own god to lead you or provide for you. It says plainly that only a fool makes his or her own god, and that any such man-made god is completely worthless. Isaiah 44:14, recounts "A Day in The Life of an Idol". It begins when people plant trees, and when the trees are grown, they select a sturdy oak and cut it down. With some of the wood they make a fire to warm themselves, with some, they cook their food, and then with what's left over, they make a god to worship. They bow down to it and pray to it saying "rescue us, you are our god! How ludicrous! Clearly, the creator of a thing is superior to the thing created. But amazingly, this obvious truth eludes so many people as they bow down to their self-made gods. This demonstrates that there is a need in every human heart to worship, but the sad reality is that left to ourselves, mankind will worship the things they make, instead of the one true God.

Aaron's First Choice

Aaron was a people pleaser. The Bible says that he was eloquent, but he did not use his words to speak up for God. The people said, "Come on, make us some gods who can lead us. We don't know what happened to this fellow Moses, who brought us here from the land of Egypt." And Aaron said, okay! He did not say, "Why do you need any gods? Jehovah is your God", nor did he ask them how a god they make can be depended upon to lead them. He also did not correct their misconception about Moses. Moses was not their god, he did not bring them out of Egypt, he was merely the leader that God used. Aaron did not ask any of these pertinent questions to help the people recalibrate, and to lead them away from their terrible idol idea. He failed woefully in his role as God's representative. He made a choice to please people rather than God.

Before we judge Aaron harshly, let's consider ourselves. First Corinthians 5 says that we are God's ambassadors on planet earth. He has left us here to represent Him and His kingdom, and He said to us, "occupy till I come." But how many times have we kept silent when we should have spoken up? How many times have we been poor representatives of God? How many times have we let the fear of people, what they will say, their disapproval, persecution, or ridicule - keep us from doing what we know is God's will?

Aaron committed a terrible sin in making the golden calf. The Bible says that when the people saw the calf, they exclaimed, "O Israel, these are the gods who brought you out of the land of Egypt!" The moment he heard the people ascribe to the golden calf the praise that was due to God alone, that should have been his clue to realize that what he had done was wrong. Aaron knew too well that it was not this calf that brought the Israelites out of Egypt. Yahweh did!

For starters, the chronology was wrong. They had been out of Egypt for a while now, and they just made this calf. So, how is it that a calf they just made delivered them from Egypt? Aaron knew this, but, instead of speaking up against this madness, he doubled down in his sin. When he saw how excited the people were, he built an altar in front of the calf. Then he announced, "Tomorrow will be a festival to the Lord!" That begs the question, Which God, Yahweh or the golden calf? Aaron was blinded by the people's praise. He thought he could mix and mingle the worship of the golden calf with the worship of Almighty God. But God is very clear. He had said, "you shall have no other god beside me". But Aaron, who should know better, misled the people. The next morning the people sacrificed burnt offerings and peace offerings to the calf. After this, they celebrated with feasting and drinking, and indulged in pagan revelry.

This sorry spectacle is what happens when a person who claims to be a Christian lives like the world. When they do, they mislead and confuse people. First Peter 2:9-10, says that we, like Aaron, are priests of God. We are chosen by God, chosen for the high calling of priestly work, chosen to be a holy people, God's instruments to do His work and speak out for Him, to tell others of the night-and-day difference He made in and for us, moving us from nothing to something, from rejected to accepted. So, when we smoke weed, party, engage in extra-marital sex, pornography, and money worship, we abuse our priestly office and lead people down the path of hell and destruction. They don't know better, but we do. The truth is that whether you know it or not, people are watching you, and the way you live your life impacts and influences others.

In 1 Kings 12, we read of another leader who made golden calves and led the Israelites away from God. His name was Jeroboam. He was a man that God had raised from obscurity and poverty to become king of the ten tribes of Israel. But after God made him king, he decided that the only way to remain king was to keep the people from going to Jerusalem to worship God at the temple. The Bible says that "Jeroboam thought to himself, "Unless I am careful, the kingdom will return to the dynasty of David. When these people go to Jerusalem to offer sacrifices at the Temple of the Lord, they will again give their allegiance to King Rehoboam of Judah. They will kill me and make him their king instead." So, on the advice of his counselors, he made two golden calves. Then he said to the people, "It is too much trouble for you to worship in Jerusalem. Look, Israel, these are the gods who brought you out of Egypt!" He placed one calf in Bethel and the other in Dan, at both ends of his kingdom. But this became a great sin, for the people worshiped these idols." This sin brought judgement and destruction on Jeroboam and his family.

Aaron's Second Choice

Many times in life, we look at those who have a high office in the church or in the culture, and we think that they have it all together. But that is not the case. Aaron had a high office, but he blew it big time! When Moses went up to the mountain to meet with God and left him in charge, he made a golden calf for the Israelites and led them into idol worship. God told Moses what was going on and directed him to go down quickly from the mountain to address the situation. When Moses came down, he was angry. He took the golden calf, burned it in the fire, ground it into powder, threw it into the water and forced the people to drink it.

Then He said to Aaron, "What did these people do to you to make you bring such terrible sin upon them?" What was Aaron's response? He chose to blame the people, lie, and disclaim responsibility. He said to Moses, "You know how evil these people are. They said to me, 'Make us gods who will lead us. So, I told them, bring me your earrings, and when they did, I simply threw the earrings into the fire, and out came this calf!"

Instead of repenting, asking God for forgiveness, and taking personal accountability for his failure, Aaron blamed the people, but made no mention of his own culpability in agreeing with their proposal and giving them a plan to execute it. He then proceeded to lie. He said that he simply threw the earrings into the fire and out came the calf. But the Bible says differently. It says that Aaron took the gold earrings, melted them down, and molded it into the shape of a calf. Aaron diminished his key role in this idolatrous escapade.

Sadly, playing the blame game is a popular human sport since the beginning of time. We saw it first played in the garden of Eden when Adam blamed Eve for his disobedience to God. We also saw it in 1 Samuel 15:15, when Saul, the king of Israel, blamed the people for his disobedience to God. He had disobeyed God's express command to completely destroy the Amalekites. Instead, he and his men saved the best of everything for themselves, and when he was confronted by the prophet Samuel, he said, "The army spared the best of the sheep, goats, and cattle to sacrifice them to the Lord your God. We have destroyed everything else." Blaming Eve did not work for Adam, blaming the army did not save Saul, and blaming the people did not exonerate Aaron!

In the face of Aaron's failure, Moses made a call for leadership courage in the camp. He said "All of you who are on the Lord's side, come here and join me." And all the Levites gathered around him. Moses told them, "This is what the Lord says: Each of you, take your swords and go back and forth from one end of the camp to the other. Kill everyone, even your brothers, friends, and neighbors."

The Levites obeyed Moses' command, and about 3,000 people died that day. Think of it, Aaron's disobedience and failure resulted in the death of 3000 people in one day.

When Moses made the call, "Who is on the Lord's side?" The Levites rose to the occasion. They cleansed the land of the idol pollution and avenged God's honor. Then Moses told the Levites, "Today you have ordained yourselves for the service of the Lord, for you obeyed him even though it meant killing your own sons and brothers. Today you have earned a blessing.

Obedience Broke the Curse!

Aaron was a Levite. Where he failed, the other Levites succeeded and earned a blessing from God. But the Levites were probably the last tribe one would expect to arise and excel in this way. Their grandfather, Levi, had been cursed for a transgression in his youth. In Genesis 49:5, when Israel was about to die and was blessing his sons, instead of a blessing, Levi got a curse because of an incident recorded in Genesis 30. His sister, Dinah, had been sexually violated by Shechem, the son of a Canaanite king, who really liked Dinah and wanted her for his wife. But God had told the Israelites not to inter-marry with the Canaanites. Well, Levi and his brother Simeon were justifiably angry about the violation of their sister. But what they did about it, is what earned them a curse. The Bible says, "be angry, but sin not", but Levi committed a grave sin in his anger. He and Simeon tricked the men of Shechem into believing that they would allow their son to marry Dinah, but only if they agreed to be circumcised like the Israelites. So, the men of Shechem agreed and were circumcised. Then, while they were still in pain and unable to fight, Simeon and Levi massacred them all! Their fury was so great and destructive that their father cursed them for it.

He said: "Simeon and Levi are two of a kind; their weapons are instruments of violence. May I never join in their meetings; may I never be a party to their plans. For in their anger they murdered men, and they crippled oxen just for sport. A curse on their anger, for it is fierce; a curse on their wrath, for it is cruel. I will scatter them among the descendants of Jacob; I will disperse them throughout Israel." (Genesis 49:5-7 NLT).

Those were powerful words, and generational curses that would have hindered the progress of Levi and his descendants throughout their lifetime. Levi must have felt like a marked man. By all appearances, he was doomed to a life of mediocrity, laboring under a curse. But thank God that Levi's story did not end in Genesis. As we read on into Exodus, we find that Levi had two grandsons, Moses and Aaron, who, in spite of the curse, were called, anointed, and mightily used by God. Moses became the greatest leader of the nation of Israel, who led them out of slavery and gave them the law; and Aaron became the first high priest who brought God's people into His presence, foreshadowing Christ our eternal High Priest.

The story of Levi fills me with hope. It tells me that with God, nothing and nobody is too far gone. He always has a plan of redemption, and He can turn things around on a dime! With Him there is always mercy and grace, and, it is never over until He says so. So, if the odds are against you today, if you are laboring under a curse, bondage, addiction, or a situation that appears impossible, never give up. Turn to God and He will redeem your situation for your blessing and His glory. He is the God of the second, third, and as many chances as you need.

In the case of Levi, it gets even better. When the descendants of Levi answered Moses's call, their action not only reversed the generational curse on their tribe, it consecrated them for the service of God, and earned them a blessing. In Numbers 25:6-13, the Israelites again sinned against the Lord, and engaged in sexual immorality and the worship of Baal. Then, as everyone was weeping before the Lord for this sin, Zimri, a leader from the tribe of Simeon brought a Midianite woman into his tent, right there in front of Moses and the whole assembly. When Phinehas the grandson of Aaron saw this, he jumped up, took a spear, went after the man and killed both him and the Midianite woman. Then the Lord said to Moses, "Phinehas, because of this zealous act, has turned my anger away from the Israelites. So, tell him that I am making my special covenant of peace with him. I give to him and his descendants a permanent right to the priesthood."

In the face of Zimri's brazen immorality, Phinehas, the grandson of Aaron, took action to honor God. Because of that, the curse on Levi and his descendants was completely reversed, and instead of a curse, God made an everlasting covenant of peace with them.

In Malachi 2:5-6, God gives us additional insight about this covenant. He said that, "The purpose of my covenant with the Levites was to bring life and peace, and that is what I gave them. This required reverence from them, and they greatly revered me and stood in awe of my name. They passed on to the people the truth of the instructions they received from me. They did not lie or cheat; they walked with me, living good and righteous lives, and they turned many from lives of sin.

Levi and his descendants did not settle for life with a curse overhang. They sought God, walked with God, and took action to honor God, and that not only broke the curse, it reversed it and brought them a mighty blessing and everlasting covenant!

Levi's and Aaron's stories are stories of redemption, and they should give you hope that regardless of what has transpired in your life, you can still turn it around. The key is to walk with God and honor Him. So, if you have messed up big time, no big deal! With God's help, you too can fix it. Like Levi and Aaron, you can go from a big mess up, to an eternal covenant and permanent priesthood.

CHAPTER 2
MIDDLE EAST GREED

BALAAM

In October 2020, a District Judge in Upstate New York sentenced a 60-year-old man to 120 years in prison. The convicted man was Keith Renaire. He was the leader of Nexium, a self-help organization which he claimed, offered the keys to higher consciousness. His organization attracted the rich and famous, including movie stars and heiresses to multi-billion-dollar fortunes. According to the prosecutor, Renaire's promised goal was to "actualize human potential and offer members a new ethical understanding." But in reality, he created a secret society which recruited women as sex slaves.

Stories like this make us wonder what went wrong? How did a group that started out with what appears to be lofty ideals, end up with sex slavery; and why would very intelligent, wealthy, and accomplished women allow themselves to become sex slaves? Well, the key is in the power of teaching and persuasion. Renaire was described as unassuming yet very persuasive, so much so that he was able to lure many famous, educated and accomplished women into modern day sex slavery. Keith Renaire's choices and decisions had tragic consequences, not only for him, but for so many other people. His story was featured on the television series, American Greed.

There is a man in the Bible whose story is like Keith Renaire's. Like Renaire, his story is about money and sex, and his choices and decisions also had tragic consequences for so many. I think that if there was a "Middle East Greed" Television series, he would be featured there as well. This man's name is mentioned in four books of the Bible, and every time, it is followed by a warning. This is because his choices and teachings have devolved into an insidious doctrine that has infiltrated and defiled the church. In Revelation 2:14, Jesus Himself calls this man out by name and warned the church about him and his doctrine. Jesus told the church in Pergamum that this man's evil doctrine had crept into their church, and He warned them to "Repent…., or I will come to you suddenly and fight against you with the sword of my mouth."

Jesus is the Lord of the church. Can you imagine Him fighting against a church? Life is hard enough when you have God on your side. Imagine having God fighting against you. In Matthew 16, Jesus said, I will build my church, and the gates of hell shall not prevail against it. But here we see that this man's doctrine is so destructive, that Jesus Himself will fight against any church that allows, tolerates or accommodates that doctrine. And how will Jesus fight against them? With the sword of His mouth. The word of God is the best, and most effective weapon against evil. The word of God is the truth and will always expose and overcome the lies of the devil.

Jesus is not the only one who warned us about this man and his doctrine. In 2 Peter 2, apostle Peter warns us about this same man and his evil teachings. In a long paragraph talking about false teachers, this man is singled out by name, and apostle Peter warns us not to follow his footsteps, because he loved to "earn money by doing wrong". The Message Bible describes him as "the prophet turned profiteer, a connoisseur of evil."

So, the Lord Jesus warned us about this man, and apostle Peter warned us about him as well. But that is not all. Jude, the half-brother of Jesus also warns us about this man and his teaching. Jude is a one-chapter book, with only 25 verses, and yet this man's deception was so destructive that Jude mentioned him by name and calls him out as a person who deceives people for money. So, who is this man, what is his doctrine, and why is it so destructive?

Balaam and Balak

His story is in Numbers 22. The Israelites had left Egypt and had wandered in the wilderness for forty years. Now they were finally at the shores of the promised land. They were camped by the Jordan river, across from the city of Jericho, in the plains of Moab. When the people of Moab saw the Israelites, they were terrified. They had heard about the great and mighty things God did for Israel, how He delivered them from Egypt, fought their enemies, and provided for them in the wilderness. So, Balak the king of Moab, decided that he had to do something. He knew that he couldn't overcome Israel in a fair fight, so he came up with a plan to weaken and destabilize them. He sent for a prophet named Balaam. This man had a great reputation as a prophet. It was believed that whoever he cursed, was cursed and whoever he blessed was blessed. So, Balak invited Balaam to come and curse Israel for him. He believed that if Balaam cursed Israel, then he will be able to conquer them and drive them away from the land. He promised to pay Balaam a lot of money.

When Balak's officials arrived and gave Balaam the message, he told them to spend the night, so he could pray about it, and in the morning, he would tell them what the Lord says. Now, think about it. Balaam was supposed to be a prophet of God, and he was invited to curse the people of God, and he wanted to pray about it. What is there to pray about? You would expect Balaam to immediately say, "Absolutely not! I cannot curse God's chosen people." He knew the Israelites were God's people, so, why in the world would he be willing to even entertain the idea of cursing the people of God? The answer is greed. Balak promised him a lot of money and Balaam wanted the money and prestige that he would get from this assignment. We don't know what was going on in his life at this time. Maybe he needed to make a new addition to his home, or maybe Mrs. Balaam needed a new donkey. Whatever was going on was enough to make prophet Balaam open to the idea of cursing the people of God for financial gain! Contrast that with the response of apostle Peter in Acts 8, when a man named Simon offered him money in exchange for the power of the Holy Spirit. Peter and John had come to Samaria to minister. Simon, saw how they laid hands on people and they received the Holy Spirit. So, he offered them money saying, "let me have this power too, so that when I lay my hands on people, they will receive the Holy Spirit." Peter didn't say, "Let me pray about it". Rather, He rebuked him sharply and said:

"May your money be destroyed with you for thinking you can buy God's gift! Your heart is not right with God. Repent of your wickedness and pray to the Lord to forgive you". As a result, Simon immediately repented, and asked Peter to pray for him. The result of Peter's firm response is that God was honored and Simon learned a valuable life lesson, that you cannot buy the gift of God with money. But Balaam is different. He was willing to entertain the thought.

Sadly, what Balaam did is what many Christians do when they lust and desire for things that are outside God's will. They know what the word of God says, but they are looking for a loophole. They are looking to find a way to justify doing what they know is against the will of God. This is one way Christians open the door to the devil in their lives and let sin develop in their heart. Our first reaction every time we are tempted to do something outside the will of God should be an immediate and emphatic NO! We should not consider it, or even allow the thought to linger for a minute. Our response should be "Absolutely not, end of story." But many times, Christians allow sinful desires to simmer in their minds and occupy their thoughts. They think about it long and hard enough, until they find a way to rationalize what they know is wrong.

As children of God, we must be on the alert and watch out for the lures and temptations of the devil to step outside the word of God to meet our needs. This is a favorite and very effective strategy of the devil. During a time of pressing need, he brings pressure on you to compromise your Christian principles to meet that need. The problem is that if you yield to his temptation, you may solve that one problem, but you end up creating other bigger problems, and most importantly, you lose fellowship with God. Also, once you step outside the will of God to get what you want, now you have to stay outside His will to keep it. God has promised to provide our needs. Many times, His timing is different from ours, and the devil tempts us to seek alternative means to meet that need outside of God. So, we must be watchful, especially in times of stress and need. We must determine in our hearts to say No to the devil's lure every time.

Balaam and The Lord

Balaam had told the officials of Moab to stay the night and he would give them the answer from the Lord in the morning. But we don't find Balaam praying or asking God about the invitation from Moab. In fact, it was God who came to him and asked him, "who are these men visiting you?" This shows that Balaam had not gone to seek God about King Balak's request. It also indicates that Balaam already knew what God's answer would be, and so he did not bother to ask. He knew that God would say No, but he wanted to go to Moab, and he was trying to figure out how to achieve that goal.

God's question to Balaam is noteworthy. When God asks you a question like that, it's an indication that you are in trouble. It's the same type of question He asked Adam in the garden of Eden. He asked, "Adam, where are you?" It's also the same type of question He asked Elijah when he was hiding in the cave. God asked him, "What are you doing here Elijah?" These types of questions from the Lord are not seeking information. They are questions to call you to attention and self-awareness; to open your eyes and make you reconsider where you are and what you are doing.

Well, Balaam told the Lord about the invitation from Balak to curse Israel and God told him clearly, "Do not go with the messengers. You are not to curse Israel because they are blessed." The next morning, Balaam said to the messengers, "go home, the Lord will not let me go with you". So, they left. However, when they got back home and told king Balak, he would not take "no" for an answer. He decided to try again. This time, he sent a bigger and even more distinguished delegation, and promised Balaam even more money.

When the upgraded delegation came back to Balaam with king Balak's more lucrative invitation, he said to them, "Even if Balak were to give me his palace filled with silver and gold, I would be powerless to do anything against the will of the Lord my God."

That sounds pretty good. Balaam had said "No, I will only do what God tells me to do. But the problem is, he didn't stop there. He then told them to, "stay here one more night, and I will see if the Lord has anything else to say to me." Now, why would he say that? What has changed from the first delegation to this one? The request has not changed. King Balak still wanted him to curse Israel, and he had already asked God about that and God clearly told him not to go. The only thing that changed is that Balak's delegation is bigger and better, and that he had promised Balaam more money. We know that the money and the upgraded delegates would not move God or change His mind, so asking God again will not achieve a different result. However, Balaam's response showed that he was moved by the distinguished officials and the promise of even more money. The stature of the delegates made him feel very important and more money was exactly what he wanted. Balaam was in the tight, unrelenting grip of greed and pride. So, instead of sending the delegates back with what he already knew was God's answer, he stalled because his heart was enticed. He wanted to go with them and was trying to find a way to get God to allow him to do what he wanted to do. James 1 explains the process of sin's seduction. It states that, "Temptation comes from our own desires, which entice us and drag us away. These desires give birth to sinful actions, and when sin is allowed to grow, it gives birth to death." Balaam was hooked by king Balak's lure.

This is a sober lesson for us. How many times has God told you to do something – maybe give some money to the church, or help a person or family in need, or take better care of your body by exercising, and instead of obeying God, you said, like Balaam, "let me pray about it" and by the time you finished your "praying", you have talked yourself out of doing what God told you to do. One TV pastor joked that when he gets the urge to exercise, he sits down and thinks about it, until the urge passes. This may be a funny joke about exercise, but the real life consequences of disobedience to God is not funny at all. Partial obedience or saying to God, "let me think about it" is disobedience.

This story of Balaam illustrates one of the devil's most successful strategies, the strategy of repeat temptation. When the enemy brings a temptation to you the first time, and you say "No", he doesn't go to hell and lick his wounds. He tightens the pressure on you. For example, in a temptation to compromise your biblical convictions for financial gain, maybe you were already behind financially, and he offered you an opportunity to compromise your principles for money, and you said "No". He then tightens the noose. Maybe your car breaks down, or a new unexpected bill arrives in the mail and increases your need and stress level. Then he presents the temptation again. Now the stakes are higher, and it's looking a lot better than it did the first time. Now you are more likely to justify compromising your principles to meet these pressing needs.

This strategy applies, not only in the area of finances, but in other areas as well. I have seen instances where single Christians who said "No" to premarital sex early on in their season of singleness, are pressured by the devil to compromise when they have been single for a long time. The enemy pressures them with the fear that their "body clock" may run out and they may not be able to have children anymore, or he terrorizes them with the thought that they may be alone for the rest of their lives unless they are willing to compromise their standards. In Luke 4, when the devil tempted Jesus, and Jesus defeated him, he didn't just go away and suck his thumb. The Bible says that he left Jesus until "a more opportune time". We have an enemy who is relentless. He wants to destroy us, and repeat temptation is one of his favorite tactics. He uses repeat temptation to wear you down, repeat disappointment to break your spirit and drive you to despair, and repeat discouragement to turn you against God and make you believe that God doesn't love you. We must ask God for help to stand strong against him.

Balaam's First Choice

Balaam really wanted to go with the officials of Moab. So, he told them to stay the night so he can ask God again, if He really meant what He said the first time. If you have small children you know exactly what is going on here. When you've told your child that they can't have that cookie, but they come back again and again, asking if you really meant to say "No". Their goal is to wear you down until you change your "no" to "yes". They really want that cookie and they'll keep asking until they get it. Sometimes, they play both parents against each other. Mom says "No", so they go to dad and ask. Of course, they don't tell dad that mom had already said "No". All they want is for dad to say "Yes" so they can have that cookie. As a Christian counselor, I see this in counseling. Some people don't want the truth, and they don't want to get better either. So, they keep shopping for counselors until they find one that tells them, not the truth, but what they want to hear.

Getting a second opinion is a good idea when you are dealing with doctors, but not when you are dealing with Almighty God. God's word is true and when we question and second guess the word of God, it is evidence of a heart focused on sinful desires. This type of lustful persistence is driven by the flesh and exploited by the devil. It's the same strategy he used in the garden of Eden to deceive Eve. He came to her and said, "Did God really say?" In today's culture, questioning the word of God is at an all-time high. Many Christians have been convinced by popular culture that the word of God is outdated. They want to modernize God and bring Him up to date. They want a God who changes with the times and whose standards can be adapted to fit their ever changing lifestyles. So, they constantly ask, "Did God really say?" They find it hard to believe that a holy God, would tell us to be holy, that a righteous God would tell us to flee from sexual immorality, and that a good God would tell us to reject hate, bias, and prejudice. They deceive themselves into believing in a make-believe God. Someone has said that in the beginning God made man in His own image, and since that time, mankind has been trying to return the favor.

Well, in the case of Balaam, he went back to God to ask again, and this time, God said to him: "go with the men, but do only what I tell you to do." Balaam had got his way! The next morning, he saddled his donkey and started off with the men from Moab. What the Bible says next may sound contradictory or even shocking, but it is not. Numbers 22:22 says that God was angry that Balaam was going, so he sent the angel of the Lord to stand in the road to block his way.

You may be thinking, why was God angry with Balaam? After all, He gave him permission to go? Well, this is the danger of wanting something so badly, that you are willing to question or compromise the word of God to get it. It's a classic case of "Be careful what you ask for, because you might get it". When it's your way or the highway, God can let you have your way, but the consequences can be dire! In the Bible there are several examples of times when people wanted something so badly, and asked for it so many times that God let them have what they wanted and it brought destruction to them. Psalm 106:14-15 tells the story of when the people of Israel craved meat in the wilderness. They repeatedly complained that they had no meat to eat, and fantasized about going back to Egypt where they had "flesh pots". So, God gave them what they asked for, but sent leanness into their souls. One translation says that they got what they asked for, but along with it they got an empty heart.

You see, some of the things we want can empty our heart of love for God, and compassion for people. Some people have wanted money so much that when they got it, it emptied their heart of faith, and they began to rely on money to do for them, the things that God did. They began to rely on money to protect them, provide for them, and be their security. Little by little, money took the place of God in their lives. In Mathew 6, Jesus warned us about this snare. He said, "you cannot serve God and money".

Some people have craved romantic relationships so much that it emptied their hearts of their biblical convictions, morals, and self-respect. They pull God off the throne of their hearts and put that man or woman there, and elevate their desire to please this person over their obedience to God and His word. Some other people have wanted power and popularity so much that it emptied their hearts of their biblical worldview, faith, and commitment to God's word, truth, righteousness and justice.

In the case of the children of Israel, they wanted meat so badly that it emptied their hearts of reverence for God. They glorified their time of slavery in Egypt and despised all the mighty things that God had done to set them free. The story is in Numbers 11. They craved for meat and complained, saying, "We remember the fish we used to eat for free in Egypt. And we had all the cucumbers, melons, leeks, onions, and garlic we wanted." They developed selective amnesia. It is true that they ate fish in Egypt, but it was not "for free". They were not free. They were brutally oppressed slaves, and their male children were murdered, but now, in their craving, they had forgotten that the food of Egypt was not free at all; it had a terrible cost.

Their complaining got to Moses, and he was discouraged and cried out to God: "Where am I supposed to get meat for all these people?' God told Moses that he would feed the people with meat for a whole month, and He did! God sent them a mountain of quails. The people went out and gathered meat all day long. But while they were gorging themselves on the meat, while it was still in their mouths, the anger of the Lord blazed against them, and He struck them with a severe plague and they died. The Bible tells us in 1 Corinthians 10, that these things are recorded as a warning for us, lessons that teach us not to fall into the same temptation of craving for evil things. Meat is not evil, but wanting it so badly that you complain and dishonor God is. You see, God is able to provide and supply all our needs. So, the need is not the problem, the bad attitude is! They could have asked God for meat and He would have provided for them, if they asked in faith. But instead, they lusted and complained.

The Mercy of Unanswered Prayer

Sometimes, we need to thank God for the things we don't have, and the prayers that He did not answer. You see, how we handle the times when God says "No" to our prayers tells a lot about who we are, what we know about the character of God, and how much we trust Him. Apostle Paul had unanswered prayer. In 2 Corinthians 12, the Bible tells us that he pleaded with God three times to remove a "thorn in the flesh" that tormented him, but God said "No". Instead, of removing the problem, God said to him, "My grace is sufficient for you, my power works best in weaknesses". Apostle Paul trusted God enough to accept His "No", not with a defiant and dejected attitude, but with a humble and obedient heart. Instead of letting unanswered prayer steal his joy, he flipped it and chose to rejoice. He stopped hiding his "thorn" problem, being embarrassed about it or pretending that it doesn't exist. Rather, He began to boast gladly about his weakness, so that the power of Christ can work through him. He said, "I began to take pleasure in my weaknesses, and in the insults, hardships, troubles, and persecutions that I suffered for Christ." This is because he realized that when he admitted his weakness and inadequacy before God and leaned on Him, he became strong in God's supernatural strength.

Jesus also had unanswered prayer. In the garden of Gethsemane, He prayed passionately with tears that God would remove the cup of suffering from Him, but there was no other way to save fallen humanity. So, He accepted God's 'No", and went to the cross to pay for the sins of mankind. You and I can learn from these examples. We can learn to trust God when He says "No". We can learn to thank God for protecting us from what we thought we wanted, and giving us what He knew we needed.

Balaam and the Talking Donkey

In Balaam's case, he went off with the Moabite delegation, but God was angry with him, and so, He sent an angel to stand in the road to block his passage. What the Bible says next is jaw dropping! "Balaam's donkey saw the angel of the Lord standing in the road with a drawn sword in his hand to kill Balaam. So, the donkey bolted off the road into a field, but Balaam beat it and turned it back onto the road. Then the angel of the Lord went and stood at a place where the road narrowed between two walls. When the donkey saw the angel of the Lord, it tried to squeeze by and crushed Balaam's foot against the wall. So, Balaam beat the donkey again. Then the angel of the Lord moved farther down the road and stood in a place too narrow for the donkey to get by at all. This time when the donkey saw the angel, it lay down under Balaam. Balaam beat the donkey again. Then the Lord gave the donkey the ability to speak with a human voice, and it asked Balaam a question: "What have I done to you that deserves your beating me three times?" Wow!

Sometimes, we read things like this in the Bible and act like this is normal. But it is not. This is crazy, and I am not the only one who thinks so. Apostle Peter speaking of this incident, said that a dumb donkey spoke with a human voice and restrained the "prophet's craziness." A donkey speaking with a human voice is crazy! If you are curious like me, you might wonder whether the donkey spoke with a male or female voice, or whether it spoke Hebrew or Aramaic? But one thing is sure, this donkey did not speak donkey. God gave it the ability to speak human words, words that Balaam could understand. I wish they had smart phones back then. Someone would have caught a video of this bizarre spectacle and posted it for us to see. This is super powerful! Our God is Almighty. Nothing is too hard for Him to do.

Child of God, this story should encourage you, and fill you with awe and reverence for our Omnipotent God. This story illustrates the point that God will stop at nothing to make His word and will known to us. He will speak to us in words that we can understand, and use anything, including a donkey, to open our eyes when we are blinded by our own wants and sinful desires. Today, as New Testament saints, we have the Holy Spirit living inside us, and He makes the word and will of God manifest to us. But God will also use others in our lives – our family members, godly friends, and yes, even a donkey, to tell us the truth and show us His way, if we will listen.

At the risk of sounding like "Captain Obvious" I would like to say that whenever you see abnormal things like an animal talking with a human voice, you should know immediately that something is seriously wrong; mankind had stepped out of divine order and needs to be brought back into alignment. In the garden of Eden when the snake began to talk to Eve, somehow, she missed the glaring point of a talking snake. Right there and then the light bulb should have gone off in her head and she should have said to herself, "What am I doing, talking to a snake? We don't talk to snakes!" That would have ended the Satanic conversation right there, but instead she carried on a full conversation with a snake without even realizing that something was seriously wrong. We see the same thing with Balaam. The talking donkey should have alerted him immediately to the fact that he was gravely out of order. He had owned this donkey for a while and never before had it spoken with a human voice. So, this abnormality should have been a flashing red signal to Balaam to stop. But amazingly, he missed it completely and carried on a full conversation, in public, with a donkey, yelling at the donkey and issuing threats of bodily harm to the donkey.

What about you? What will it take to get your attention? In Luke 19, Jesus said that if human beings would not praise God, the stones would immediately cry out in praise. You and I were not in the garden of Eden for the snake talk, and we were not in the field with Balaam for the donkey talk, but Jesus says that if our generation will not praise him, we would witness a new low - stone talk. While a talking snake and a talking donkey are extremely bizarre, at least they are living things. But if our generation does not praise God, He will give a mouth and breath to stones and they will erupt in jubilant praise. In case you haven't figured it out, stone talk is much worse than donkey talk. It doesn't get colder or deader than a stone. When someone is completely devoid of feeling, we say that they are "stone cold". Can you imagine how terrible stone praise would sound? Can you imagine how much power it will take to warm up a stone, give it a mouth and breath to proclaim God's praise? May we never see that day! I am determined to praise God daily. Psalm 150 says, "Let everything that has breath praise the Lord". Do you have breath? I invite you to join me in making a personal commitment to praise God daily. As long as we have breath, you and I, there will be no stone praise in the earth, not on our watch!

For Balaam, donkey talk did not faze him at all. He talked right back to the donkey. He shouted at the donkey "You have made me look like a fool!" "If I had a sword I would kill you!" The donkey answered, "But I am the same donkey you have ridden all your life," "Have I ever done anything like this before?" "No," Balaam admitted.

Can you imagine this spectacle? Balaam shouting at his donkey? This is why apostle Peter called him a crazy prophet. His only focus was that the donkey made him look like a fool in front of the distinguished Moabite delegates he wanted so much to impress. The sad irony is that his life was at stake, but he was completely oblivious to that fact. For Balaam, his reputation and how he looked to people was all that mattered. It doesn't matter what or who he actually is, just how he looked. And, if you read the transcript of the conversation recorded in the Bible, the donkey made a lot more sense than the prophet. I wonder what the Moabite delegation thought when they saw Balaam yelling at his donkey. All his efforts to look good in front of these people have failed and they see him as the crazy prophet that he is, and he blames the donkey for his humiliation.

This is how foolish you and I look when we are trying desperately to please people. Only God knows the crazy things we have done in order to fit in, to be accepted, to be liked, and to look good in front of people; the lies we have told, the principles we have compromised, the times we have not spoken up for truth or the times when we stood by and allowed injustice to happen or remain, simply because we did not want to offend people. Balaam's story is a cautionary tale for us. We must make pleasing God our highest priority and trust Him to manage our reputation with people. This is what Jesus did. Philippians 2:7 says that He "made Himself of no reputation". Knowledge of who He was freed Him from human opinions, good or bad, and released Him to fulfill His mission. We must do the same. We must not look to people for approval, validation, acceptance or applause. We must not draw our self-image or identity from other people. Our self-image and identity must come from God alone. His opinion is the only one that matters, and He already loves, accepts, and approves of us, and nothing can change that.

Balaam and The Angel

As Balaam was shouting and threatening his donkey with bodily harm, the Lord opened his eyes, and he saw the same thing his donkey saw. He saw the angel of the Lord standing in the roadway with a drawn sword to kill him, and he did exactly what the donkey did. He bowed his head and fell down on the ground before the angel. The angel said to him, "Why did you beat your donkey those three times? Look, I have come to block your way because you are stubbornly resisting me. Three times the donkey saw me and stayed away; otherwise, I would certainly have killed you by now and spared the donkey."

Wow! Did you hear that? The angel rebuked Balaam for beating his donkey; said that by going on this journey, Balaam was stubbornly resisting God; that his stubborn resistance was deserving of death, and that he would have been dead but for the donkey. The donkey saved his life!

If you had asked Balaam at any time before his confrontation with the angel, he would have confidently said that God had given him the approval to go with the Moabites. Meanwhile, all the time, he was being driven by his lust and was actually stubbornly resisting God by his willful desire to go. This tells us that we can deceive ourselves to believe whatever we want, and that because the door has opened for something we want, does not necessarily mean that it is from God. We must seek God Himself for direction and clarity. It also tells us that our willful resistance and questioning of the integrity of God's word is a serious matter, deadly serious.

Here we have a prophet so filled with his own wants and desires that he was blind to spiritual truth and spiritual warfare going on all around him. Balaam is a prophet, but a dumb donkey was smarter and more spiritually aware than he was. The donkey saw the angel, but the prophet did not. Balaam was blinded by his desire for money, prestige, and human acclaim that he was in mortal danger and did not even know it. If the donkey had not taken the initiative, Balaam would have been spiritual roadkill.

The lesson is clear, being consumed with our own desires can give us blind spots on the road of life. It can make us oblivious to dangers that are right in front of us. We can be so fixated on getting what we want that we miss the red flags warning us of danger. This type of tunnel vision is a favorite strategy of the enemy and has destroyed the lives of so many. As a Christian counselor, I have seen this again and again in the lives of God's people. Several years ago, a young man going through a bitter divorce told me with deep regret, how sinful tunnel vision ruined his life. He confessed that the desire for premarital sex had blinded him to glaring red flags and issues in his girlfriend that eventually ended up destroying their home and marriage. Another young woman confessed to me how God warned her about a man she was dating, but she had to have that man, and so, she went ahead, only to find out, too late, that he was living a double life. May the Lord help us to say "No" to unbelief and willful rebellion, and to submit to His word, will, and plan for us.

Prophet Balaam was so out of touch with God, that his donkey had better spiritual perception than he did. Donkeys are not very smart animals. They are literally called dumb. Yet this man's donkey was smarter than he was, so much smarter that he rebuked the prophet with a human voice; and so smart that the angel would have killed the prophet and let the donkey live. We must take a personal inventory and ask God to show us areas of rebellion in our lives that are in opposition to His plan and purpose. We must ask God to help us to keep a light grip on the things of this world; to look to Him as our source, and not to people; and to be alert and awake spiritually so we are not spiritual roadkill on the highway of life.

This brings us to an interesting point. If God can speak to a man, and a prophet through a donkey, He certainly can speak to a man through a woman! Some churches believe that women cannot teach or preach the word of God to men. Well, Balaam's donkey begs to differ. The truth is that God will use whomever He chooses to speak His word. In John 4, He used the "woman at the well" to spread His word to the men of Samaria, in Judges 4, He used Deborah to lead Israelite men into battle, in John 20, He used Mary Magdalene to spread the good news of His resurrection, and in Acts 2, He promised to pour out His spirit on all flesh, men and women alike, to prophesy or declare His word. God will stop at nothing to make His word and will known to us. He will use anything or anyone, including female preachers, to tell us the truth and show us His way; and a man who will not listen to a woman will end up listening to a donkey!

Honest Doubt or Rebellion?

There is a big difference between honest doubt, seeking confirmation from God, and questioning the integrity of God's word. We must not be afraid to come to God with our honest doubts and questions. He welcomes them and will gladly help us to understand. He knows that His ways are higher than our ways and His thoughts, higher than our thoughts. So, He is ready and willing to teach us and help us to overcome our honest doubts. Jesus' disciple Thomas is famous for his doubts and questions, but every single time, Jesus took the time to answer his questions and help him to get over his doubts. In fact, some of the most powerful revelations of Jesus that we have in the Bible came from His answers to doubting Thomas.

In the same vein, God is not offended or intimidated by our seeking confirmation from Him. Judges 6 tells the story of Gideon and his many requests for confirmation from God. God never once rebuked Gideon, rather, He provided confirmation after confirmation to help Gideon get over his fear. God welcomes our honest questions and doubts, but He has a problem with our willful resistance, unbelief or questioning the integrity of His word. We see this in Luke 2, when Zechariah the priest questioned the message of angel Gabriel that his wife Elizabeth with give birth to John the Baptist. The angel took Zechariah's unbelief so seriously that he struck him dumb, so that he was unable to speak until the baby was born.

Someone has said that the difference between doubters and unbelievers is this: Doubters look for reasons to believe, unbelievers look for reasons not to believe. Doubters ask questions, unbelievers refuse answers, God accepts doubters, but He rejects unbelievers.

Balaam in Moab

When confronted by the angel, Balaam confessed. He said, "I have sinned. I didn't realize you were standing in the road to block my way. I will return home if you are against my going to Moab." The angel told Balaam, "Go with the men from Moab, but say only what I tell you to say." So, Balaam went on with Balak's officials."

When Balaam arrived in Moab, king Balak went out to meet him. He scolded Balaam for not coming right away when he sent for him, and reminded him that he would reward him richly for his service. The next morning, he took Balaam up to a hill from where he could see the Israelites camped below, and told him to curse Israel. When Balaam stepped away to seek God's direction, instead of a curse, God gave him a blessing for Israel. So, Balaam came back to Balak and his officials, and spoke this prophecy:

Balaam's First Prophecy

"The king of Moab brought me from the eastern hills to 'curse Jacob and announce Israel's doom.' But how can I curse those whom God has not cursed? How can I condemn those whom the Lord has not condemned?" (Numbers 23:7-8).

This prophecy was certainly not what king Balak had asked for, and he was furious. He said to Balaam, "What have you done to me? I brought you here to curse my enemies, the Israelites, but instead, you have blessed them!" Balaam replied, "I will speak only what the Lord puts in my mouth."

If you belong to God, this should rejoice your heart! This is your inheritance as a covenant child of God. The Bible says, over and over again, that you are blessed, and so, you cannot be cursed. Almighty God has already blessed you and your blessing is irreversible. Regardless of what the devil and his agents say or do, no hex, curse, incantation, or witchcraft can succeed in your life. None! Anyone who sets out to curse you, will turn around and bless you instead.

This reminds me of the story I heard of a young man who had been a devil worshipper for almost 25 years. He met a girl he really liked. This girl was raised in church but had stopped going to church when she left home, but her parents continued to pray for her. The young man's plan was to date her and bring her into Satan worship like he had done with so many other girls before her. But week after week, he could not convert her to Satanism. She wasn't going to church anymore, but yet she wasn't coming over to Satanism either. Finally, in frustration, during one of his devil worship sessions, the young man asked the devil, "Why can't I get this girl?" The devil said, "Her God has said that she is untouchable." Hallelujah! if you are a Christian parent out there and your gave your child to God and they have walked away from the faith, don't give up! Continue to pray for them. Your prayers make them untouchable to the enemy.

Balaam's Second Prophecy

King Balak did not give up his quest to curse Israel. He said to Balaam, "Come with me to another place. There you will see another part of the nation of Israel, but not all of them. Curse at least that many!" So, he took Balaam to a plateau overlooking the camp of Israel, and again invited Balaam to curse Israel, but God would not allow it. Instead of a curse, Balaam declared this blessing:

"God is not a man, so he does not lie. He is not human, so he does not change his mind. Has he ever spoken and failed to act? Has he ever promised and not carried it through? Listen, I received a command to bless; God has blessed, and I cannot reverse it! No misfortune is in his plan for Jacob; no trouble is in store for Israel. For the Lord their God is with them; he has been proclaimed their king. No curse can touch Jacob; no magic has any power against Israel. For now it will be said of Israel, 'See what wonders God has done for them! (Numbers 23:19-23).'

This prophesy of Balaam is one of the most beautiful and reassuring portions of scripture. It outlines key foundational truths and attributes about the nature and character of God; attributes that should give you and I tremendous confidence in our great God.

1. First it tells us that God is not a man. This might appear to be an obvious statement, but many times we tend to forget that God is not a man. In fact, comparing God to man is one of the key strategies of the devil to lie to us and discourage us. Many times, the devil works in the lives of Christians to make us resentful toward God. He accuses God in our

hearts. He whispers to us, "If God really loved you, why did He let that happen to you? Why did He not deliver you from that terrible situation? If God really cares, why did He let you go through that? Think about it, if it was your child and you had all the power to stop anything bad from happening to them, wouldn't you? If you could keep them from all that pain, wouldn't you? God doesn't love you, He doesn't care, and He cannot be trusted to take care of you." And sadly, we listen; we listen to the devil's taunts because it makes sense to our natural minds. And we agree with the devil and conclude that God doesn't care. A related Satanic strategy is to make us view the love of our perfect heavenly Father through the lens of the flawed love, imperfections, and failures of our earthly fathers.

The disconnect is that we are expecting God to act like a human being and we are judging him by human standards. The problem is that God is not a man. Today's scripture states that very clearly. So, accusing God of not acting like a human being to deliver you, the way you would act to deliver your natural child, is completely missing the point that God acts with a perspective far beyond what any human being can see, or understand. God's vantage point is not just your particular life and circumstance, but all of humanity, all of time and all of eternity. Isaiah 55 emphasizes this point. It states that God's ways are higher than our ways and His thoughts are higher than our thoughts. God is not a man and we should be thankful for that! One singular proof that God is not a man is that He sent His only Son to die for sinful, rebellious mankind. I do not know of any human being who would willingly subject their child, talk less of their only child, to horrendous torture and death like the one Jesus endured on the cross, to save others. God is not a man, and thank God that He isn't! If God were a man, we would still be in our sins, and condemned to death.

2. Secondly, Balaam's prophecy tells us that our God is unchanging. God is not fickle like human beings. He does not change his mind on a whim. We live in a time when people's words mean absolutely nothing. Someone can tell you that they will do something, and simply not do it, and when you ask them about it, they act like it's not a big deal. Unfortunately, it is a big deal. Our words matter. You see, we live in a word-based universe. Our world was created by words and responds to words. God created the world with words and He created us like Himself. So, our words have power. When we fail to honor our words, it diminishes us tremendously. It tells our hearts that our words have no power. Then when you are sick and you pray and speak to your body to be healed, it does not obey you. The reason is because you have taught your body that your words are meaningless. It is sad to see how Christians, who for years speak powerless and meaningless words, suddenly want their words to count when they speak to their kids or when they need healing or something else from God.

3. Thirdly, Balaam's prophecy tells us that God keeps His promises. He has never spoken and failed to act. He has never promised and failed to carry it through. So, we can completely trust Him and rest in His faithful love and

character. In creation, God spoke the world into existence, and set the heavens in place. Since then, all of creation is kept and sustained by the word of God. The heavens have never caved in on the earth, they are held securely in place by the invisible pillars of the spoken word of God. Our words have the same power. If we would keep and honor our word, we have the power to create our future with our words.

I like the old western TV shows. They were set at a different time, when a person's word was their bond. In the words of Chester Good in Gunsmoke, "A man ain't worth much if he can't keep his word." So, people would make a deal, shake hands on it and it is sealed. They simply honor their word and do not go back on it. In Lonesome Dove, a cowboy gave his word to his dying friend, that he would carry his dead body back to his Texas hometown for burial. That man traveled hundreds of miles in a wagon, fought off Indians, animal predators, scavengers, faced insurmountable obstacles, and almost lost his own life to keep his promise to his dead friend. Every time he stopped over in a town along the way, the townsfolk would try to convince him to bury the body there. After all, he had done his best and had suffered so much. But again, and again, he would refuse and remind them that he gave his word. Eventually, he did succeed in taking that body back to Texas and buried under the tree just like he promised his friend. We live in a different world today, a world where people make promises they don't intend to keep. Romans 1:31 tells us that one of the signs of a godless, depraved society that has abandoned God, is that people will become untrustworthy and break their promises.

You and I can choose to be different from today's culture, and determine to reflect the character of God by being faithful and true, no matter what.

4. Fourthly, Balaam's prophecy tells us that God's blessings for His people are irrevocable and irreversible! It is not in the nature of God to bait and switch. God does not bless you and then say "Oops, I did not mean to say that". God is not Santa Claus. He does not bless you based on whether you've been naughty or nice. God is not fickle. Romans 11:29 captures this divine attribute. It says that "the gifts and calling of God are irrevocable." This means that when God blesses you, you are blessed period! Ephesians 1:3 states that in Christ, God has blessed us with every spiritual blessing, and 2 Peter 1:3 says that by His divine power, God has already given us everything we need for living a godly life. We are already blessed! We don't need to pray, fast or plead for God's blessing. God has blessed us, and nobody can revoke or reverse it! We just need to believe the word of God and walk in our inheritance rights as the blessed people of God.

One of the most ineffective prayers we can pray is to ask God to bless His children. This is because we are asking God to do what He has already done. The reverse is also the case. Because God has already blessed us, he cannot un-bless us. This means that nothing you can do today will stop God from loving or blessing you, because He already has. Don't allow the lies, guilt and condemnation from the devil to rob you of fellowship with your heavenly Father. God loves you with an everlasting love. No matter what you've done, run to Him for mercy and receive His eternal love and care.

5. The fifth proclamation from Balaam's prophecy is that no misfortune is in God's plan for Jacob; no trouble is in store for Israel. If God said that concerning Israel under the old covenant, imagine our portion under the new covenant! Hebrews 8:6 states that the covenant we have in Christ is a better covenant, established upon better promises than the covenant God made with Abraham. So, this promise applies much more to us. God's plans for us are good plans. There is no misfortune, calamity, evil, or destruction in God's plans for us. One of the devil's most oppressive tactics is fear. He holds men and women in bondage through fear; fear of the unknown, fear of the future, fear of harm, failure, death, and so on. Some people live with a continual, evil foreboding, a feeling that something bad will happen. It's like they are waiting for the other shoe to fall. Their lives are ruled by an irrational, generalized fear, a fear of something, anything going wrong. This spirit of fear robs them of their joy and peace. But this type of fear is based on a lie! It is the complete opposite of what God promised His children. In Jeremiah 29:11, God said, "For I know the plans I have for you, "They are plans for good and not for disaster, to give you a future and a hope." So, whose report will you believe, God's or the devil's? I challenge you today to believe God. Refuse the voice of fear, reject the thought or expectation of misfortune and harm, and embrace the great future that God has planned for you. Only believe and you will receive!

6. The sixth declaration in Balaam's prophecy is that the Lord our God is with us; and he has been proclaimed our king. We do not need to fear! We are never alone. Another translation says that the Lord our God is with us and the shout of a King is among us. The Bible says that where the word of a king is there is power. The King of kings lives in us and He has given us His word of authority and power. First John 4:4 states that He who is in us, is greater than he who is in the world. In Hebrews 13:5-6, God promises that He will never leave us, forsake us, or abandon us. "So, we can say with confidence, "The Lord is my helper, so I will have no fear. What can mere people do to me?" When Jesus is your King, you have nothing to fear. God is able to take the very worst things that happened in your life, and make them work together for your good. We cannot outrun, out-grow, or out-sin the love and grace of God.

7. The seventh proclamation from Balaam's prophecy is that no curse can touch us, and no magic has any power over us. We do not need to fear witches, wizards, hexes, spells or curses. So many Christians are afraid of the devil, his demons and their agents. But that fear is based on yet another lie, the lie that the devil has limitless power to harm you. In Luke 10:19, Jesus said, "Look, I have given you authority and power over all the power of the enemy, and you can walk among snakes and scorpions and crush them. Nothing will injure you." Note that Jesus has already given us power and authority over the devil and his kingdom. The devil has power, but his power is rogue. He has no authority to exercise that power in the life of a child of God. Unlike the

devil, believers in Jesus have both power and authority. Authority is the power to command, and Jesus said that we can exercise His authority over snakes and scorpions. Here the Bible is not just referring to literal snakes and scorpions, but is speaking about the devil, his demons, and agents. We have authority in the name of Jesus to trample and crush them under our feet.

The devil has no authority over you, but he is a liar and a thief. He will try to deceive you into giving him your authority or tell you lies that make you open the door to him through fear. This is why Ephesians 4:27 warns us to give no room to the devil. As long as we say "No" to the enemy, he has no right, power, or authority over us. James 4:7 makes the point clearly. It tells us to submit ourselves to God, resist the devil and he will flee. To overcome, all we have to do is to stand in the finished works of Christ, and shut the door on the devil.

8. The eight proclamation from Balaam's prophecy is that our lives will showcase the wonders of God. Balaam prophesied: "So now it will be said of us, 'See what wonders God has done for them!' What a powerful proclamation of the unqualified favor and goodness of God to His people! First Corinthians 2:9 confirms this prophecy. It states that "No eye has seen, no ear has heard, and no mind has imagined what God has prepared for those who love Him". We are God's trophies, to display His power, love, grace and goodness to the world. Ephesians 3:10 states that "God's purpose was to use us to display his wisdom in all its rich variety to the devil, his demons, and all the unseen rulers and authorities in the

heavenly places" and Ephesians 3:20 states that He is able to achieve infinitely more than our greatest request, our most unbelievable dream, and exceed our wildest imagination. He will outdo them all for His miraculous power constantly energizes us. Hallelujah!

Here's the bottom line, God wants to be good to us. He scours the earth daily for an opportunity to fill out lives with His goodness. Second Chronicles 16:9 states that, the eyes of the Lord run to and fro throughout the whole earth, to show Himself strong on behalf of those whose heart is loyal to Him. God wants to show up and show off on our behalf. In Jeremiah 33:3, He says, call upon me and I will answer you, and show you great and mighty things that you did not know. God is a good, good, Father. He is our Abba, and the Shepherd of our souls. If you are a child of God, look up! God loves you and wants to be good to you. His goodness and mercy are chasing you down. So, it will be said of us, you and I, 'See what wonders God has done for them!'

Balaam's Third Prophecy

After Balaam's second prophecy, King Balak was mad! He said to Balaam, "Fine, but if you won't curse Israel, at least don't bless them!" and Balaam replied, "I can only do what the Lord tells me to do." Then Balak decided to try one last time. He said to Balaam, "Come, I will take you to one more place. Perhaps it will please God to let you curse Israel from that location." So, he took Balaam to the top of Mount Peor, overlooking the wasteland." But there again, instead of cursing Israel, God commanded Balaam to bless His people, and Balaam prophesied:

"How beautiful are your tents, O Jacob; how lovely are your homes, O Israel! They spread before me like palm groves, like gardens by the riverside. They are like tall trees planted by the Lord, like cedars beside the waters. Water will flow from their buckets; their offspring have all they need. Their king will be greater than Agag; their kingdom will be exalted. God brought them out of Egypt; for them he is as strong as a wild ox. He devours all the nations that oppose him, breaking their bones in pieces, shooting them with arrows. Like a lion, Israel crouches and lies down; like a lioness, who dares to arouse her? Blessed is everyone who blesses you, O Israel, and cursed is everyone who curses you." (Numbers 24:5-9)

God of the Mountains and Valleys

It is important to emphasize that if you are a child of God, His blessing on your life, is not dependent on your location or station. King Balak, tried to get Balaam to curse Israel from different locations because he was under the mistaken belief that location can stop or cancel God's blessings. Deuteronomy 28 says that as a child of God, you are blessed in the city, and blessed in the field, blessed going out, and blessed coming in. Wherever you go and whatever you do, you are blessed. God's blessing, power, and goodness in your life is not locational. It is secured by covenant, attaches to your person, and goes with you wherever you go, unless of course, you disobey God and go to a place God told you not to go. People who don't know the God of the Bible, think that He can be limited by time, space, or location. They think that Yahweh is like the pagan gods and goddesses that have a geographical domain or sphere of influence. But the God of heaven is not like these idols. He is the Lord Almighty, unlimited, and uncut, and He rules and reigns supreme over all the earth. Psalm 24:1 proclaims the eternal truth, that the earth is the Lord's, and everything in it.

A story in the Bible illustrates this point! In 1 Kings 20, Ben-Hadad, king of Aram attacked the nation of Israel. He assembled his entire army, as well as thirty-two other kings, and besieged Samaria. He demanded that king Ahab surrender his wealth, wives, and children to him. Initially, Ahab agrees, but when Ben-Hadad added another condition, that he and his servants will take anything that they laid their hands on, Ahab refused. Ben-Hadad was mad, and threatened to completely wipe out Samaria. Then a prophet of the Lord came to Ahab and told him that God will give Israel victory over the Arameans, and he gave Ahab God's strategy for the battle. Ahab obeyed God, and the Lord gave Israel a resounding victory! They crushed the king of Aram and the 32 kings allied with him.

To explain their defeat, the Arameans said that the God of Israel was a God of the hills and that was why Israel was stronger than they were in Samaria. They proposed to Ben-Hadad to fight Israel again, but this time, in the valley; with the expectation that they will prevail. Once again, the prophet of God came to King Ahab and told him that Ben-Hadad's army will strike again in the spring: and then he prophesied that 'Because the Arameans think that the LORD is a god of the hills and not a god of the valleys, God will deliver Ben-Hadad and his vast army into the hands of the Israelites.

In the Spring, it happened just as the prophet said. Ben-Hadad came back with his huge army and fought Israel in the valley of Aphek, but God gave Israel a mighty victory! Ben-Hadad's forces were defeated so thoroughly in the second battle, that he surrendered to Ahab. God gave Israel victory both at Samaria in the hills, and at Aphek in the valleys to show that, unlike the idols and finite gods of Canaan, Almighty God is sovereign over all territories and regions of the earth. Our God is the God of the mountains and the valleys. He is the all-powerful, infinite Ruler of the whole earth.

King Balak is about to learn the same lesson that king Ben-Hadad learned. That the God of heaven is the omnipotent King over all the earth, and that His power, blessing, and favor on His people are not locational. God's people are blessed because God has blessed them and nobody can curse them.

Lessons from Balaam's Third Prophecy

There are many lessons that we can learn from Balaam's third prophecy about the awesome plan and purpose of God for His people.

1. First, Balaam proclaimed that God's people are like palm groves. Psalm 92:12-14 echoes this comparison. It states that, "The righteous shall flourish like a palm tree... Those who are planted in the house of the Lord shall flourish in the courts of our God. They shall still bear fruit in old age; they shall be fresh and flourishing,"

   The palm tree provides a powerful image of a productive and fruitful life. There are different varieties of palm trees, and every single one is useful. Take for example the oil palms. Every part of the oil palm tree is used and useful. The fresh palm fronds are used for making baskets, mats, and roofs for thatched houses. The dry palm fronds are used as wood for cooking and heating; the palm fruit can be roasted and eaten as a snack, or crushed and pressed to produce rich, red palm oil for cooking. Palm oil is also used for making soaps, shampoos, personal care, hygiene, and cleaning products, makeup, lotions, and more. In addition, palm oil is used for industrial processes and to produce biodiesel. After oil production, the spongy remains of the crushed fruit are used as sponges for household cleaning, and as kindling for fire. The palm kernels inside the fruit are cracked and the cracked shells are used for road paving in place of gravel, the kernel nuts themselves are eaten as a delicious snack or pressed to produce palm kernel oil, which is used for personal grooming, cosmetics, and as oil for lighting, heating, and industrial processes. The left over hash from the crushed kernel nuts are used to produce animal feed. I can go on and on. Every part of the oil palm tree is extremely valuable, productive, and fruitful. So much so, that the oil palm tree contributes significantly to the Gross Domestic Product of many tropical countries and to the economy of the world. God wants every Christian to flourish like the palm tree, and to be fruitful in every season of life.

Also, the palm tree is a symbol and picture of resiliency. Most of us are familiar with the TV images of hurricane devastated coasts and neighborhoods where the only thing standing is the palm tree. It has an uncanny ability to survive adversity and extreme high force winds. Many palm tree trunks are spongy and flexible, they bend, but do not break. This is why, during a hurricane, the palm tree can bend over until it's parallel to the ground, and then when the storm passes, it will rise back up until it's standing straight and tall. The palm tree's root system contributes to its resiliency. It has many short roots that spread out over layers of soil, helping the tree to secure a lot of soil in its "grip", which keeps it stable. Also, palm trees are not burdened by heavy branches. Their trunks are free and clear, and all the branches are at the top, providing a great shade and canopy, but also relieving the tree trunk of the weight of heavy branches. When strong winds of adversity blow, the palm tree bends and lets the wind stream through its canopy of leaves, but it remains standing after the wind is gone.

God wants us to be as resilient as the palm tree. Jesus said, "In the world, you will have trouble, but be of good cheer, I have overcome the world." In Matthew 7, He taught us to be intentional in how we build our lives, because the rains of adversity will fall, the rivers of life will rise, and the gale force winds will blow, but like the palm tree, only the lives that are resilient will remain standing after the storm.

In addition, palm trees are a powerful symbol of faith and triumph. In Judaism they represent peace and plenty. The Romans gave palm branches to the triumphant champions of games and wars as a symbol of victory. One week before His crucifixion, Jesus rode triumphantly into Jerusalem, and was welcomed by large crowds waving palm branches and proclaiming, "Hosanna! Blessed is he who comes in the name of the Lord. Blessed is the coming kingdom of our father David! Hosanna in the highest heaven!" Jesus' purpose was to make public His claim to be the Messiah.

God wants us to put our faith on display as salt and light to our world, like the waving palm branch. John 4:4 says that, every child of God overcomes this evil world, and our faith is the victorious power that triumphs over the world. God wants us to live by faith daily, and to crown Jesus king in our lives.

2. Secondly, Balaam proclaimed that God's people are like gardens by the riverside. In agrarian Bible societies, the ability to grow crops for food is dependent on the availability of water, and an entire nation can be wiped out by famine if there is a drought. In these cultures, gardens by the riverside are a treasure. They are lush, green, and productive all year round. God is saying that in Him, we are like gardens by the riverside, lush, plush, and well supplied. In John 15, Jesus said, I am the vine, you are the branches. If you abide in me and my word abides in you, you will bring forth much fruit. Psalm 1 echoes that promise. It says that the person who honors, obeys and delights in God is "like a tree planted by the rivers that bears its fruit in its season, its leaf does not wither, and whatever s/he does shall prosper."

If you are a child of God, you are in Christ. That means that God has transplanted you from death to life, from darkness to light, and from the curse into the blessing. Colossians 1:13 states that "God has rescued us from the domain of darkness and transferred us into the kingdom of His dear Son, who purchased our freedom and forgave our sins." In Christ, we are standing firm, like a flourishing tree, planted by God's design, deeply rooted by the river of God, bearing fruit in every season of life, never dry, never fainting, ever blessed and ever prosperous in all we do. This is our heritage as the people of God. So, no matter where you are in your life journey, or what you see right now in your present circumstances, I challenge you to believe God. Believe that you are a tree of righteousness, planted by God Himself beside the rivers of living water. No matter how bad things look, choose to stand on the word of God and you will emerge victorious, fruitful, triumphant, and prosperous like a well-watered garden by the riverside.

3. Next, Balaam proclaimed that God's people are like tall trees planted by the Lord. The prophet Isaiah made the same proclamation. In Isaiah 61:1-3, he prophesied: "The Spirit of the Lord God is upon Me, Because He has anointed Me to preach good news to the poor; He has sent Me to heal the brokenhearted, to proclaim liberty to the captives, and freedom to the prisoners...to comfort all who mourn...to give them a crown of beauty instead of ashes, the oil of festive joy, instead of mourning, the garment of praise instead of despair; that they will be called trees of righteousness, planted by the Lord, that He may be glorified."

In Genesis, when God created the first trees, He spoke to the earth. He said, "Let the earth produce vegetation: seed-bearing plants and fruit trees..." and the earth produced the trees. God did not plant the trees. He simply spoke and they came into being. But here, He declares that His people, are like tall trees, not spoken into being like in Genesis, but planted by the Lord Himself.

What God is saying is that He is mightily at work in our lives. However tough or overwhelming your situation is, God wants you to know that He is doing some gardening in your life. He is calling forth the tremendous future and destiny that He sees in you. Are you physically sick? Are you struggling with emotional bondage or trauma? Are you incarcerated in prison, or bound by an addiction, wrong mindset, or bad habit? Are you grieving some personal, financial, or relationship loss in your life? Are you depressed, discouraged, or emotionally downcast? God is asking you to look up. This is not the end of your story. He is working in your life to bring beauty out of your ashes. He is cultivating and planting in you, tall trees, trees of righteousness.

Go outside and look at all the beautiful trees and plants that God created. If He created all this simply by speaking to the earth, imagine the beautiful, stately, majestic trees that He can produce when He takes the time to personally select and plant. You are God's select tree, a tree of righteousness, standing tall and strong, displaying the glories and excellencies of God to planet earth.

The Gardener

In John 20:15, Mary Magdalene saw the risen Christ and thought that He was the gardener, then He called her by name and she knew immediately that it was Him. She recognized His voice. It was the same voice that had planted faith in her heart, and cultivated hope in her spirit; the voice that had set her free from demonic oppression and bondage. It was the voice of the Gardener who planted and nurtured the life of God in her soul.

Mary was right. Jesus is indeed the Gardener. He was the Gardener who created the garden of Eden. Colossians 1:16 states that He was the creator of all things and in Him all things hold together. He is Mary's Gardener! Under His loving care, Mary, the demon possessed woman, tormented by seven demons, had become a tall tree of righteousness. She became so tall and so strong that she followed Jesus everywhere. She did not care about the whispers and negative opinions of others. She did not let shame, reproach, stigma, or the disapproval of other people stop her extravagant worship of her Lord. "She was present at the mock trial of Jesus, she heard Pontus Pilate pronounce the death sentence; and she saw Jesus beaten and humiliated by the crowd. She was one of the women who stood near Jesus during the crucifixion."

On resurrection morning we see Mary again. Mary loved Jesus so unconditionally, and was so totally committed to her Savior that she got up early that Sunday morning to go and anoint His body. The wonder of it all is that she thought He was dead. Now, anybody can love and follow a living Jesus, a Jesus who does miracles, a Jesus who feeds thousands, and a Jesus who walks on water. But Mary got up that morning to love on a Jesus she thought was dead. Her passion for her Gardener was not limited to the good times. It transcended the cross and the grave. Once again, she did not let anything or anyone stop her. There was a huge boulder at the entrance of the tomb. She was not strong enough to move it, but she did not let that stop her. She went to the tomb anyway. She believed that somehow, God would make a way, and He did. Mary's love and worship for the Gardener of her soul knew no limits, and because of that, she became the very first person to witness, see, and talk to the resurrected Christ!

What is Mary saying to you and I today? First, she is challenging us to rekindle our love for Christ. In Revelation 2, Jesus rebuked the church in Ephesus because they had forsaken their first love for Him. Mary is saying the same thing. She is saying to us: "Love the Lord Jesus, with all your heart, soul, and might. Love Him with every breath, and every fiber of your being".

What does your love for the Savior cost you? Is your love for Jesus vibrant and extravagant? Do you worship Jesus only when He is performing miracles and doing great things in your life, or will you, like Mary, still worship Him when He appears to be dead, ineffective, silent, and absent? Will you, like Mary, still go to the graveyard of your dreams and unanswered prayers to worship Him?

Secondly, Mary is saying to us, "Do not give up, do not lose hope, this is not the end of your story. Give the Gardener a chance to finish His work in your life". Wherever you are in your Isaiah 61 journey; whether you are at the prison stage, the despair stage, the mourning stage, or the ashes stage, God's ultimate goal is to get you to the tree of righteousness stage. This is when your life looks so different from what you have been through that nobody would believe it if you told them. That is evidence of the Gardener at work, bringing forth beauty out of your ashes.

4. Fourthly, Balaam prophesied that God's people will have water flow from their buckets. In the land of Israel, both in Bible times and even today, water was and is a precious commodity. Water was literally the difference between life

and death. An abundance of water meant life, food, and prosperity, and a drought literally meant famine and death.

In John 4, the Bible tells the story of Jesus talking to a woman at the well of Samaria. He asks her for water and then tells her that He can give her living water, such that she will never thirst again, and will never have to come to the well to draw water. Jesus said to her, "whoever drinks from the water that I give will never thirst again. In fact, the water I will give will become in him a well of water springing up for eternal life." Jesus was talking about spiritual water, the refreshing water of the Holy Spirit in the soul, bubbling up to eternal life. Do you have this water?

This is not the water that you can buy or pipe. It comes from the well of the Spirit, deep within your innermost being. It doesn't matter how much money, fame, or clout you have. If you don't have this water, your life will fall apart, your money will do no good and your fame will leave you desperate and alone. You see, everything else, money, fame, and clout are external, but this water comes from the well of the spirit, deep within you. It is not controlled by anything external, people cannot take it away from you, and after the fame and clout is no more, this water will sustain you through every season and challenge of life. It will take you through the mountains and the valleys, and will be there when you step into eternity. Do you have this water?

The Holy Spirit

In John 7:37-39 the Bible records that, "On the last day, that great day of the feast, Jesus stood and cried out, saying, "If anyone thirsts, let him come to Me and drink. He who believes in Me, as the Scripture has said, out of his heart will flow rivers of living water." But this He spoke concerning the Spirit, whom those believing in Him would receive; for the Holy Spirit was not yet given, because Jesus was not yet glorified."

Jesus is making the same offer to you and I today. The good news is that for us, on this side of the cross, the Holy Spirit has been given. He is God, just as the Father and the Lord Jesus. He lives inside every genuine believer and can overflow inside you with His living water. Do you have Him? If you haven't received the Holy Spirit, you can receive Him today.

In Acts 19:2, apostle Paul asked believers in Ephesus "Did you receive the Holy Spirit when you believed?" And when they said "No", he prayed for them and they were baptized in the Holy Spirit, and began to speak in other tongues or languages. God wants to do the same for you. In Acts 2:17-18, He promised that, "In the last days, I will pour out my Spirit upon all people; and in Mark 16:17, Jesus said, "These miracle signs will accompany those who believe: they will drive out demons in the power of my name. They will speak in tongues." This promise is for you. You can receive the outpouring of the Holy Spirit right now, simply by asking God to baptize you with His Holy Spirit. In Luke 11:13, Jesus said that if we, as human parents, know how to give good gifts to our children, how much more will God give the Holy Spirit to those who ask Him. So, let's ask Him! To receive the baptism of the Holy Spirit, pray this prayer:

> Lord Jesus, you are the one who baptizes with the Holy Spirit. I ask you now to baptize me with your Holy Spirit - Amen!

Now open your mouth and speak your new prayer language! Keep in mind that you receive the person of the Holy Spirit the same way you received Jesus, by faith. There are no fireworks, goose bumps, or magic feelings. Simply believe that you received when you prayed, then open your mouth and speak, not in your native or a learned language, but in the new language given to you by God. Note that God will not open your mouth for you and "make" you speak in tongues, just as He will not open your mouth for you and make you speak in English or any other known language. You have to open your mouth in faith and speak.

You may feel silly speaking a language you don't understand, but don't let that stop you. You are speaking to God spirit to spirit, and Romans 8:26 says that God understands exactly what the Holy Spirit is saying through your lips, because He prays for you according to the will of God. Just like any other language, your proficiency in your new prayer language will grow with practice. So, continue to speak in your new language every time you pray, and see the power of God unleashed in your life!

5. The fifth proclamation from Balaam's third prophecy is about our children. God said that the children of His people have all they need, and that they will spread life everywhere they go. This is a declaration that we can boldly speak over our children, that they will have no lack, and will minister the life of God to their generation. God is massively invested in the

lives of our children. He has anointed them to prosper and empowered them to succeed in the earth. In Psalm 112:1-3, He said "Blessed are those who fear the Lord, who delight greatly in His commandments. Their children will be mighty and powerful on earth; the generation of the upright will be blessed. Wealth and riches will be in their house, and their righteousness endures forever." Then in Isaiah 49:25, He promised to fight with anyone who fights with us and to save our children. Also, in Isaiah 54:13, He said that all our children will be disciples taught by the Lord and obedient to His will; and that we and our children shall be far from even the thought of oppression, destruction, fear, and terror, because it shall not come near us. This is our heritage as the people of God.

Are you worried about your children? Do you have children who have wandered away from the Christian foundation you laid for them? Do you have a child bound by alcohol, pornography, marijuana, or other addictions? Don't despair. God is massively invested in the lives and future of your children, and He is working in their hearts and lives to bring transformation. Turn your children over to Him. Believe His word, and say out loud, "My children shall be mighty upon the earth. God has broken every form of bondage in the lives of my children. God is discipling my children. He is their mentor and is teaching them by His Spirit. He will conform them to His will, purpose, and destiny for their lives in Jesus' name. Amen."

6. The sixth proclamation from Balaam's third prophecy is that: "Their king will be greater than Agag; their kingdom will be exalted. God brought them out of Egypt; for them he is as strong as a wild ox. He devours all the nations that oppose them, breaking their bones in pieces, shooting them with arrows. Like a lion, Israel crouches and lies down; like a lioness, who dares to arouse her?"

This is a compelling proclamation of God's presence, protection, deliverance, and victory for His people. We as God's people, are prosperous and strong. God is our defense and refuge by day and night. The Lord will overpower our enemies and crush all those who rise up against us. They will come out against us in one way, and flee in seven ways. We will possess the gates of our enemies, because the Lord our God is our Savior and Deliverer. Hallelujah!

David said in Psalm 118, 'The Lord is on my side; I will not fear. What can people do to me? ... It is better to trust in the Lord than to put confidence in people...You pushed me violently, that I might fall, but the Lord helped me. The Lord is my strength and song, and He has become my salvation. The voice of rejoicing and salvation Is in the home of the righteous; The right hand of the Lord does valiantly. ... The right hand of the Lord is raised in triumph. I shall not die, but live, and declare the works of the Lord.'

Child of God, whatever battle you are facing today, whether it's a legal battle, a battle against a terrible sickness, or a financial battle, the Lord will fight for you. The battle is not yours, the battle is the Lord's. He will fight for you and give you victory. The arm of God will fight your battles, the voice of God will speak for you and be your advocate, the name of the Lord will be your defense by day and by night, the presence of God will make a way for you where there seems to be no way, and the finger of God will bring counsel and direction into every area of your life. God will make roadkill out of your enemies like He did to Pharaoh and his army.

7. Balaam concludes his 3rd prophecy with a forceful declaration. He said, "Blessed is everyone who blesses you, O Israel, and cursed is everyone who curses you." Hallelujah! If you are a child of God, not only are you blessed, but God wants you to be an example and distributor of His blessings. Those who curse or stand against you do so at their own risk. Those who speak against you bring a curse down on themselves. God is for you, and will make a liar out of those who are against you. No weapon formed against you shall prosper, and every tongue that rises against you in judgement, you shall condemn.

Do you know that this blessing proclaimed by Balaam is the same blessing God promised to Abraham? In Genesis 12, God said to Abraham, "I will bless you and make your name great; and you shall be a blessing. I will bless those who bless you, and I will curse those who curse you...." In Galatians 3:13-14, God said that when we receive Christ, the blessing of Abraham comes upon us. This is because, when Jesus hung on the cross, He took upon Himself the curse for our sins, redeemed us from the curse of the law, and procured for us the blessing of Abraham.

After this third prophecy, King Balak "flew into a rage! He angrily clapped his hands and shouted at Balaam, "I called you to curse my enemies, but instead, you have blessed them three times. Now get out of here! Go back home! I promised to reward you richly, but the Lord has kept you from your reward." Balaam replied, "Remember what I told your messengers? I said that, 'Even if you were to give me your palace filled with silver and gold, I would not do anything against the will of the Lord.' I can say only what the Lord says!"

Then Balaam said to Balak, I am leaving, but before I do, let me tell you what God's people will do to your people in the future.

Balaam's Fourth Prophecy

Then Balaam proclaimed yet another prophecy. He said, 'A star will rise from Jacob; a scepter will emerge from Israel. It will crush the heads of the people of Moab, cracking the skulls of the people of Sheth. Edom will be taken over, and Seir, its enemy, will be conquered, while Israel marches on in triumph. A ruler will rise in Jacob who will destroy the survivors." (Numbers 24:17-19).

This is a powerful prophetic reference to the coming of our Lord Jesus Christ. A scepter is the authority to rule, and from Genesis to Revelation, the Bible speaks of Jesus having the scepter. Genesis 49:10 says that, "The scepter shall not depart from Judah, nor a lawgiver from between his feet." This is speaking of the rule of our Lord Jesus Christ who is from the tribe of Judah. In Hebrews 1:8, the Bible says of Christ, "Your throne, O God, is forever and ever; A scepter of righteousness is the scepter of Your kingdom." This is a quote from Psalm 45:6, and these scriptures proclaim Jesus as God and ruling His forever kingdom with a scepter of righteousness. Also, speaking of Jesus, Revelation 19:15, states that, "A sharp sword came from his mouth with which to conquer the nations, and he will shepherd them with an iron scepter."

So, Balaam closes out his prophecies with a proclamation of the coming Christ and His dominion and victory over Moab and all the other nations that oppose and fight against Israel. Jesus will conquer them, He will utterly destroy the enemies of Israel, while the people of God will march on in triumph. This is a sober warning to America and other nations that are being goaded by the enemies of Israel to stand against the Jewish people. The word of God is clear, those who oppose and fight against Israel will be shattered! God will thunder from heaven against them. The Message translation says that Israel's enemies will be blasted out of the sky, crashed in a heap and burned. I pray that America will continue to support Israel because God means what He says. He will bless those who bless Israel and curse those who curse them.

After Balaam's third prophecy proclaiming the coming Christ, and His authority and rule over the nations, he left Moab.

Balaam's Second Choice

Now, if Balaam had stopped here, his story would have ended very differently. He would have been known as a man who honored God and did what God told him to do. But that is not the end of the story. Balaam is presented in the Old and New Testaments of the Bible, as well as in Jewish rabbinical literature, as a wicked man who brought destruction upon the nation of Israel due to avarice. So, the question is, what happened after Balaam went back home? Well, his greed for money and the riches promised by Balak overcame his convictions and dedication to God. When the lights were out, and nobody was looking, Balaam told king Balak exactly what to do to destroy Israel. He told Balak that he did not need to curse Israel to destroy them. All he needed to do was to lure them into sin and then they would destroy themselves. In Numbers 31:16, Moses said that at Balaam's advice, Balak used the women of Moab to incite the Israelites to unfaithfulness against the Lord and they committed sexual immorality and worshiped Baal of Peor, and a plague came upon the nation. In Revelation 2, the Lord Jesus validates Moses' statement. He confirmed that Balaam told king Balak how to get the Israelites to sin against God, by enticing them with sexual immorality and food sacrificed to idols.

The incident is recorded in Numbers 25: 'While the Israelites were camped at Acacia Grove, some of the men defiled themselves by having sexual relations with local Moabite women. These women invited them to attend sacrifices to their gods, so the Israelites feasted with them and worshiped the gods of Moab. In this way, Israel joined in the worship of Baal of Peor, causing the Lord's anger to blaze against His people.' As a result of this, God sent a plague that killed twenty four thousand people. So, king Balak effectively deployed the wicked strategy of entrapment, taught by Balaam, to destroy Israel. So, what is the doctrine or teaching of Balaam?

The Doctrine of Balaam

The doctrine of Balaam consists of three parts. First, Jude, the half-brother of Jesus warned us about "the error of Balaam"; secondly, apostle Peter warned us about "the way of Balaam"; and thirdly, the Lord Jesus warned us about the "teaching or doctrine of Balaam". According to Jude 11, "the error of Balaam" was "for profit", and in 2 Peter 2:15, apostle Peter tells us that "the way of Balaam" was "loving the wages of unrighteousness"; and in Revelation 2:14, the Lord Jesus, speaking through apostle John, said that Balaam taught Balak to entice the people "to eat meat sacrificed to idols and to commit sexual immorality". So, here is the teaching of Balaam:

1. First, the doctrine of Balaam is serving God without loving God; it is a strict adherence to duty without love for God and His word. Balaam did what God told him to do, but no more. He kept to the letter of the law, but he did not love God enough to value the things that God values. Note that Balaam was a very religious man. Speaking on this point, J.C Coghlan said that, "Balaam, if he were among us, would be considered the pattern of a religious character; because he really proposed to himself a very high standard, and followed it rigidly, and to his own cost."

   Balaam maintained a high and legalistic view of God. He did what God told him to do, but only that. He did not curse Israel, because God told him specifically not to do so. But he had no qualms about teaching Balak how to entice them to sin and in so doing, to destroy themselves. He figured that it was okay to do that since God did not specifically tell him not to do that. Never mind that it achieved the same ungodly goal of the destruction of God's people. If Balaam loved God, he would not show the enemies of God how to dishonor Him and destroy His people.

2. The doctrine of Balaam, is an approach to God of resolute observance of a disagreeable rule, but not earnest obedience of a beloved parent. Balaam was like the child who outwardly "obeyed" his parent, but did not genuinely submit to their authority. Balaam wanted to go to Moab to curse Israel and receive financial gain. God allowed him to go, but did not let him curse Israel. This caused Balaam to forfeit the riches that king Balak had promised him. Balaam outwardly obeyed God, but inwardly, he was rebellious against God and His word. So, he found a way to achieve his own agenda, while still outwardly appearing to obey God. Appearances was very important to Balaam. As long as he appeared to obey God, that to him, was good enough. He forgot that God looks at the heart, not outward appearances.

3. Balaam's doctrine is serving God with the wrong motives. Balaam's motive in obeying God was not because he loved God. His motivation was a determination to escape punishment, not a desire to please God. He had a fear and performance driven motive for serving God. We see that today, when so many people treat their relationship with God like fire insurance. They get "saved" simply because they want to escape hell, not because they genuinely love God. That is the teaching of Balaam, and because of that wrong

motivation, he ended up teaching God's people how to dishonor and disobey Him.

4. The teaching of Balaam, is seeking our own will, instead of molding our will into God's will, and submitting to His will in all things. Balaam's doctrine is to desire our own will to be done, as much as possible, within the strict letter of God's commandments. Balaam wanted to go to Moab and get rich. God talked him out of it. Balaam obeyed God's will, but did not submit his will to God. He maneuvered until he found a way to achieve his own will. He said over and over again, "I would not do anything against the will of the Lord. I can say only what the Lord says!" But he ended up doing exactly what he wanted to do, which was against God's will. Balaam said the right things, but his walk did not match his talk.

5. Balaam's doctrine is a willingness to prostitute one's spiritual gifts and ministry for the "wages of unrighteousness. It is willingness to compromise biblical principles, or preach something contrary to God's word for financial gain. It is a willingness to accommodate ungodliness for greed, and to promote falsehood for financial gain. Balaam was willing to go and curse Israel for money and prestige, even though he knew that they were the people of God.

6. Balaam's doctrine is using your mouth and words to slander and destroy the people of God. It is a willingness to curse, malign, speak evil of, and spread gossip and half truths about your brothers and sisters in Christ, Christian churches,

church leaders, Christian ministries and ministers. Be careful what you say about the people of God.

7. Balaam's doctrine teaches accommodation of or making a deal with the world. Not only was Balaam willing to trade-off his own standard of truth and righteousness for money, but he used his teaching authority to persuade others to do the same. Balaam's doctrine is the belief that Christians can bargain their biblical beliefs and convictions for popularity, money, sex, or personal gain. It is the attitude that one can straddle the fence, with one leg in the world and one leg in Christ. It is the belief that Christians can live like the world with no distinction or separation. But, that is a lie. James 4:4 warns us that if we choose friendship with the world, we make ourselves the enemies of God.

8. Balaam's doctrine is a belief that a little sin doesn't hurt, especially, when there is some financial gain or personal benefit. It is a belief that the end justifies the means. In 1 Timothy 6, apostle Paul talks about this. He speaks of "men of corrupt minds and destitute of the truth, who suppose that godliness is a means of financial gain." Balaam's doctrine describes the Christians who equate the worship and blessing of God with making great sums of money. Apostle Paul warns us to keep away from people like that.

9. The doctrine of Balaam is perverting the grace of God into a license for immorality. It is the wrong mindset that, because the Israelites had an unbreakable covenant with God, they could sin with impunity. It's the same perverse attitude we

see today, where some people believe that because they are "saved" they can sin willfully and repeatedly, and simply "confess". It's the attitude that sin is "no big deal". But that is not true. As we saw in Numbers 25, the sin of the Israelites had deadly consequences. Twenty four thousand people died in one day! The consequences of willful sin are still the same even today. Balaam himself ended up dying with the enemies of God.

The doctrine of Balaam is still the devil's favorite strategy even today. He wants to get you to do his evil work for him, and destroy yourself, through sin, compromise, disobedience, and bondage. May God help us, you and I, to say "No" to this evil and deceptive doctrine every day and every time it is presented to us.

CHAPTER 3
BEHOLD EL ROI

HAGAR

The story of El Roi is the story of a young woman named Hagar. The backdrop to this story is that Abram and Sarai have been waiting, for over ten years, for the fulfillment of God's promise that they will have a son. Finally, in Genesis 16:2: Sarai said to Abram, "Since God has not seen fit to let me have a child, sleep with my maid, maybe I can get a family through her."

Sarai's frustration, disappointment, and disillusionment were real. She has prayed, waited, hoped, and believed for a son for so many years. She is now faith-fatigued. Too many false positives have eroded her confidence in herself and God's word. She is weary from her long journey of faith, and has finally decided to set up camp at a place called Town DIY (Do It Yourself). She still believes God, but her heart is weary from prolonged hoping and waiting. Sarai is at a vulnerable point! At this critical juncture, she came to a fork in the road, and decided to take the road leading to Town DIY.

Town DIY

Have you been to Town DIY? I have. It's a nice town with residents from all over the world. Many of the residents are Christians who believe the word of God, but their expectation is low, real low. They know that God's word is true, but they are guarded in their faith. They don't want to go out on a limb, because they are afraid that they may fall off and crash. They have a history of "unanswered" prayer or delayed manifestation. So, they pray non-specific prayers because they are afraid to pray bold prayers. They have smiles on their faces, but their hearts are heavy. For some, they have wept so much that they have no more tears. They are mourning the gap between where they are, and where they had hoped, prayed, believed, and expected to be at this time in their lives. Over time, years of hoping and waiting, with nothing to show for it, take a toll, and they lay down their expectancy and move to Town DIY. They serve God diligently, but do not love God as passionately as they did. The fire of God in their hearts has grown just a little cold.

Town DIY has many famous residents, including pastors, movie stars, scientists and world leaders. The devil is a prominent resident and leading citizen of Town DIY. He owns most of the businesses, appoints the sheriff, and practically runs the town. He constantly prowls the streets, day and night, like a lion, looking for easy pickings. Residents of Town DIY are his prime targets. His goal is to steal their faith and confidence in themselves and God. He wants to turn their temporary stop at his town into a permanent residency. He wants to get them to give up hope, stop trusting and waiting for God, and rather, to manufacture their own solutions and miracles. He'll make suggestions like: "Why don't you do something!" "Maybe God is waiting for you," or "Heaven helps those who help themselves."

Jesus warned us about these suggestions of the devil. In John 10:5, He told us about the voice of the stranger; He taught us not to follow that voice, because it comes only to steal, kill, and destroy. In 2 Corinthians 2, He warned us that the devil will try to take advantage of us and exploit our vulnerable moments. So, we must be alert to his evil schemes, and refuse to give him any opportunity.

Town DIY and You

What about you? Are you a current or prior resident of Town DIY? Are you weary from years of praying, waiting, and weeping? Are you standing right now at that fork in the road that leads to Town DIY?

Maybe you received a word from God and have been standing on it for a long time. But it's been so long now that God's promise sounds hollow and faint, like footsteps receding down a hallway, carrying your dreams with it. You now wonder whether you really heard the voice of God to begin with. When you want to pray and praise God, the enemy reminds you of the times and places when you had prayed and sang that same song of faith before and it's been years since, and nothing has changed. He mocks your faith.

If that is you today, I want to encourage you to leave Town DIY. Residents leave all the time. Sarai left, and I did too. We chose to reject the voice of discouragement and continue to believe God. He came through for us and He will come through for you too. The God of heaven is a good God and He keeps His promises. His timeline is often different from ours, but He will do for you what He promised.

Sarai Has A Visitor

Soon after Sarai arrived in Town DIY, she was visited by the welcome wagon. The wagon was filled with gifts and samples from the local merchants. The "pity party cake" sample tasted so good! So, Sarai placed an order. The order was delivered the very next day by the owner of the cake shop, the devil himself. As Sarai ate, she shared about her situation. The devil said to her, "I'm just trying to help you. Why do you continue to wait for God? It's already been 10 years! You are not getting any younger! You have to do something now. Maybe you can get a child through Hagar."

Sarai thought about it and it made sense to her. A son by Hagar is not the promise of God, but at least it's a child. It's much better than what she has now, which is nothing. The years of waiting, and dreaming of holding a child in her arms have taken a toll. It's too late for her now, her "body clock" has run out, but it's not too late for Hagar. Hagar can still have a child and she can hold Hagar's child and raise him as her own. What Sarai didn't realize at the time, is that the devil was showing her how to obtain God's promise without God, and outside of His divine plan.

Before we judge Sarai harshly, we must understand the tremendous pressure she was under. In her culture, bareness is a huge public disgrace and a childless woman is seen as half a woman. So, she felt like a tremendous failure as a woman. A woman's role was to have babies and keep house. If you can't do that, what good are you? Also, she carried the false, but heavy burden that she had failed Abram. She could not give him an heir. It was her fault. She felt responsible for this situation where the promise of God to Abram was not yet fulfilled, and thought that it was up to her to make it right. The devil accused her constantly with these lies over and over again. Then he told her the ultimate, but very convincing lie that giving Hagar to Abram was the "noble", unselfish, thing to do, and that she was making a "sacrifice" to give Abram what he wanted.

Sarai's Choice

Finally, Sarai succumbed to the voice of the devil, and offered Hagar to Abram as a surrogate mom. Unfortunately, Abram, unlike his prior record, did not seek the Lord or ask God for direction. He simply agreed with Sarai's proposal. After all, he too wanted a child.

As the drama unfolds, we see one of the terrible tactics of the devil as it plays out in real life. You see, when the devil tempts you to take action in self-will, he forgets to tell you that you can't control the outcome or the reaction of the other people involved. The way Sarai played out the movie in her head is this: Abram sleeps with Hagar, Hagar gets pregnant, Hagar remains the nice, obedient, little, servant girl she's always been, Hagar has a bouncing baby boy, Sarai gets to raise the baby and they all live happily ever after.

This type of arrangement was a common practice in the land of Canaan where they lived. She probably had seen it work well for other families and fully expected it to turn out great for her too, but it did not. You see, the difference is that Sarai belonged to God. She had a covenant with Almighty God, and the devil was after the covenant of God in her life. So, after he persuaded her to initiate her DIY project, he then went over to Hagar, and incited her to despise and humiliate Sarai. It's all part of his scheme to keep the promise of God from being fulfilled.

The lesson here is simple. If you have the call of God on your life, you don't have the luxury of doing things the way other people or the world does it, because you have an enemy who wants to destroy you and keep you from experiencing God's best. Your motto should be, "others may but I cannot."

It is important, as covenant believers, that we choose a life of obedience and consecration. The devil will show you examples of people who are "doing it", and tell you that it will work great for you, just like it worked for them. But the devil is a liar. What he does not tell you is that it will not work for you because his plan is to use your disobedience to destroy you and stop God's plan for your life. As soon as you step outside of God's will into sin and disobedience, now he has a legal right against you and he comes in for the kill. He can bring charges against you, indict you, arrest you, take you captive, and put you in one of his many jails - jails of pride, depression, addiction, bondage, and so on. Then, he will provoke the other people involved in the situation to exercise their own free will to take action that will destroy you.

The Characters

To illustrate, let's go back to Genesis 16 and look at the characters in this drama. First is Hagar. She was initially a victim of her circumstances. She did not choose this situation. Sometimes things happen to derail us that are not of our own doing. This is why we must be careful who we connect our lives with, because their wrong decisions can impact us. But even when you are connected to the people of God, they too can make wrong choices that could destroy you. Abram and Sarai were, by all accounts, the people of God, but they made wrong choices that negatively impacted Hagar.

Many of us know, all too well, the Hagar experience. We have been misled and disappointed by Christian leaders and ministers, people we really trusted, only to find out later that they betrayed our trust, and chose a path of sin and unrighteousness. Maybe you served under Christian leaders who were insecure and mistreated you. Sadly, these experiences are not uncommon, and they are very discouraging, but we must not let the enemy use them to lead us away from God or the church. Pastors and leaders are people too, with the sin problem and other failures that plague all human beings. The solution is simple. We cannot afford to put our trust in human beings. We must put our trust and faith in God alone.

Our next character is Sarai. Sarai was a godly woman, but she has been driven by desperation and despair to step outside of God's plan. The problem with going outside of God's will to get what you want, is that you have to stay outside His will to keep it. Now, Sarai is outside of God's will, and things haven't turned out as she expected. She has abused her authority over Hagar. Hagar was her maid and was required to obey her. She looked up to Sarai as a woman of God. So, when Sarai led her down this path of sin and rebellion, it cost Sarai her authority and credibility with Hagar.

Sarai appeared to give Hagar to Abram as his wife, but not really. To her, Hagar was only a surrogate mom. She was a slave girl with no rights or privileges, and Sarai took advantage of her, used her, and then dumped her when she didn't need her anymore.

It is a terrible feeling to know that you have just been used, especially by people you trusted, people who claimed to be the people of God; people you thought had your best interest at heart. People who told you about God and taught you the word of God. It can be a hard pill to swallow to realize that they intentionally used you for their own purposes. The feeling is one of betrayal. You wonder whether any of the things they taught you about God, and which you believed, was true. Did they really know Jesus? Then the devil, who is the real perpetrator behind all this, steps in and says: "This is unfair! Where was God when they did this to you? Why didn't He stop them? Then he tells you the ultimate lie, that these people represent God, and so, you cannot trust God either."

Abram's Choice

Our last character in this drama is Abram. Abram had been walking with God and obeying His voice for 10 years; and yet desperation, disappointment, and wanting to please his wife drove him to this terrible DIY option. Abram should have known better, but he didn't. He thought it was a good idea, or maybe he has seen Sarai so sad and depressed that he wanted to ease her pain. It could also be that Abram was as disappointed and disillusioned as Sarai, and saw this option as the way out of their misery. But they both quickly learned that not every good idea is a God idea. Getting Hagar pregnant solved one problem, the one Abram and Sarai were fixated on, but it created a new set of problems. Their fixation on having a baby had blinded them to the potential consequences of this bad choice.

That is the problem with bad choices. You can make your bad choice, but, you don't get to control the outcome or consequences of your choice. They are what they are, and most of the time, there are unexpected twists and turns that make bad choices costlier than you could ever have imagined when you made the choice.

Sarai was disillusioned with the delayed fulfillment of the promise of God, and gave her maid Hagar to Abram as a surrogate mom. Her plan was that: Abram would sleep with Hagar, Hagar would get pregnant, she would remain the nice, obedient, little, servant girl she's always been, she will have a bouncing baby boy, Sarai would raise the baby and they all will live happily ever after; but, that is not what happened. Genesis 16:4 tells us what actually happened. When Hagar knew that she was pregnant, she began to treat her mistress, Sarai with contempt."

Can you believe it? Nice, little, servant-girl Hagar became prideful! She realized that with all her beauty and money, Sarai was desperately unfulfilled. She wanted a child badly, and couldn't have one. For the first time in her life, Hagar felt like somebody! She had this one thing that Sarai has wanted and waited for all her life, and she got it with no trouble at all. So, she felt superior to her mistress. She thought that now, maybe, she will finally get some respect around here. After all, she was carrying Abram's heir! So, Hagar flaunted her pregnancy. She forgot that it was Sarai who placed her in the position to get pregnant in the first place, and if Sarai made her, she can unmake her. Hagar forgot that she was still a slave. Her pregnancy did not change her status. She forgot that Abram did not choose her to be his wife. Sarai gave her to him, but now that she has the trophy baby, she forgot Sarai.

Many of us struggle with the "Hagar syndrome". We sometimes forget the source of our blessings, elevate God's gifts above the Giver, and worship the creature instead of the creator. This is very dangerous territory to be in. It is the devil's stomping ground.

Also, Hagar's story is a case in point about the futility of envying other people. Sometimes we look at people we think have money, or fame, or status, and we envy their lives, but we don't know all the details. We don't know their secret pain and heart ache. By all accounts, Sarai was a woman to be envied. She was stunningly beautiful, so beautiful that at 90 years old, her beauty was the talk of the town and two kings wanted to marry her. She was so beautiful that her husband was scared that other men would kill him so they can have her. She was not only beautiful, she was also rich. Her husband was a multi-millionaire by today's estimates, but she was unhappy and unfulfilled. Her maid, a little slave-girl she picked up while she was in Egypt, had something that Sarai desperately wanted but couldn't have. Hagar could conceive a child.

As the dark parts of this drama take center stage, Sarai does what we do. As soon as her self-help, DIY approach backfired, she felt sorry for herself and blamed everyone else but herself. First, she blamed Abram. She said, "This is all your fault! I put my servant in your arms, but now that she's pregnant she treats me with contempt." Abram quickly disclaimed responsibility. He was not going to get in the middle of two feuding women. He said to her, "Your maid is your business. Do with her whatever you think best." Sarai's insecurity took over and she resorted to abuse, and treated Hagar harshly. Keep in mind that these are good people, God's people, but they had flaws, human flaws, insecurities, and fears, and they made bad choices too. We tend to put pastors and leaders on a pedestal. But they are just people too.

Hagar's Choice

In the face of Sarai's abuse, Hagar responded in the one way that she could control. She ran away. What she initially thought was her good fortune has turned into a nightmare. She quickly learned that she was just a "baby mama" and that Sarai was the wife.

This fiasco should sound a clear note of warning to single Christian women everywhere. Whether you are a young teen or an adult single woman, beware of the story of Hagar. So many single women have fallen prey to the temptation to have an affair with a married man. These men appear so understanding, compassionate, and supportive. Plus, they offer the prospect of security and financial stability that lures many single women. Also, they tell sob stories about how their marriage is unhappy and their wife is not meeting their needs. They fail to mention their own selfishness and the fact that instead of standing up and working through family problems like men, they run like cowards and look for comfort in another woman's arms. These men have zero commitment to anyone but themselves. It's all about them, their desires, feelings, and needs.

Unfortunately, many single women are led astray, duped or seduced into having an affair with a married man, hoping that he will leave his wife for them. The truth is that he won't! She's his wife, you are only a test drive! But, even if he leaves his wife for you, that makes you a marriage breaker, with blood on your hands. If that is what you sow, what do you expect to reap? Galatians 6:7 says that you will reap what you sow. Also, what makes you think that he will treat you any better than he treated his wife? This type of man likes toys, new, shiny, female toys. When you were sneaking around with him, the sex was secret and exciting. But when you get married, you are not new and shiny anymore, and he doesn't have to sneak around with you anymore. So, he gets bored with you and looks for the next woman, so he can sneak around with her for some exciting sex, leaving you behind.

A key lesson from the story of Hagar, is that you can't control people. When you make your own wrong choice, it rarely ever plays out the way you imagined it in your mind. People have a will and they will exercise it without reference to or approval from you or God. This is what Hagar did. She exercised her free will and ran away. As she fled, an Angel found her beside a spring in the desert. Tired, prideful, rebellious, and pregnant-out-of-wedlock Hagar is running away, and God gives her water even in the desert of her rebellion and pride. God provided for her. He gave her a refreshing spring, a place and time to stop and reflect on her life and choices.

I marvel at the grace and mercy of God! He has been watching all this drama unfold in Abram's household. He was there all the time, but nobody consulted Him – not Sarai, Abram, or Hagar. Now they have made a big mess and He shows up to help clean it up. David said in Psalm 23, "The Lord is my Shepherd, I shall not want. He makes me to lie down in green pastures. He leads me beside still waters: He restores my soul." If you belong to God, it doesn't matter where you've been or what you've done. God will never leave you or forsake you. He is your Shepherd for life. Don't listen to the voice of the devil telling you that you've messed up so badly that God will never forgive you. That is not true. Like Hagar, God will meet you, even in the desert of your rebellion. He will forgive you, restore you, and lead you along the path of righteousness for His name sake.

The Angel called her "Hagar, maid of Sarai". First, he called her by name. He knew her, even when she didn't know him. She was in the middle of the desert, far from home, tired, alone, pregnant, and not sure where she was headed or what her future holds. She probably thought nobody knew where she was and that she was all alone in the world, but God was there, and He had been there all along.

Secondly, the angel called her "maid of Sarai". He did not call her "wife of Abram". He called her who she was, not who she pretended to be or who she had deceived herself into thinking that she was. God knows you, the real you, not who you pretend to be.

The angel asked her "What are you doing here?" This is a question we need to ask ourselves periodically. It's a question about motive, purpose, and accountability. Why did you do what you did? Are you where you should be? What wrong choices have brought you out here in this wilderness all alone? It is a question that calls you to reflection, repentance, and restoration. Hagar never knew that her affair with Abram will end up leaving her stranded in the desert, pregnant, afraid, and all alone. But even "there" in that place of regret, far from home, with no prospects and nowhere to go, God came to her. He found her, provided for her and spoke kindly to her.

God asked Elijah this same question when he was on the run, afraid, depressed, and suicidal. Elijah had just been used by God to work a mighty revival in Israel. He had just called down fire from heaven, killed 450 prophets of Baal, eradicated Baal worship, and called the people of Israel to return back to God. Then Jezebel threatened his life and he ran, weary, afraid, and depressed into a cave. But the voice of God found him, even in that cave and asked him this same question, "What are you doing here Elijah?"

Wherever you are today, God is asking you the same question. What are you doing here, in this place of sin, depression, addiction, pornography, fear, worry, and anxiety? Like Hagar, He is calling you to reflection, repentance and restoration.

Hagar answered truthfully and took accountability. She said, "I am running away from my mistress, Sarai." God told her to "Go back to her mistress and submit to her authority." He also spoke into her life, and gave her a vision for her future and the future of her child. He told her that she will have a son, that he will be a wild donkey of a man, and that God will give her a great family, and descendants too many to count. He then gave her a name for the baby growing inside her, his name is Ishmael, which means, God hears. Suddenly, Hagar realized that God was there all along, that he had seen her and heard her cry in the terrible situation where she had been used, abused, and dumped by church people.

Our God hears desperate prayers. He heard Hagar's cry in the desert, and He heard Jonah's desperate cry from the belly of the great fish. If you have been crying out to God, even from the place of your mistakes and wrong choices, God hears!

EL ROI

This realization evoked a response from Hagar. She called the Lord a new name. She called Him, El-Roi: She had a personal encounter with God. She said, "in this place, I have actually seen the One who sees me. Yes! He saw me; and then I saw Him!" Her eyes were opened to see God. In this desolate place, out in the desert, on the run, God was there. He saw her, knew her by name, provided for her and gave her direction and a plan for the future. You can expect the same from God. In your place of regret, mistake, and wrong choices, you too can see God! Someone has said that God whispers to us in our pleasure and shouts to us in our pain. No matter how far you are from Him today, God sees you, knows you by name, will provide for you, and will give you direction and a plan for your future.

Like Hagar, you will discover God in a way you've never seen Him before if you will see him in your desert, and you too will give God a new name, when you experience Him in a new way. Living in Abram's house, Hagar had known God as Jehovah, but here, in the wilderness she discovered God for herself and gave Him a new name – El Roi. It's like Jesus asked His disciples: "Who do you say that I am?" Never mind what other people say about God based on their experience. You need to know Him for yourself. You need to experience God personally. You need to see Him clearly, in such a way that you can speak confidently of Him. Hagar saw Him and called Him El Roi. In Psalm 91, David said, "I will say of the Lord. He is my refuge, and my fortress, my God in Him will I trust." You can hear about the Lord in so many different ways and by so many names, but what you say of the Lord comes from personal, desert experience, like the ones David had as a shepherd boy.

El-Roi is not a name that Hagar heard from somebody else. It's a name that came from deep within her spirit. It represents the special, personal, manifestation of God in her life. She said, "He saw me and then I saw Him." He saw her and opened her eyes to see him. She may never have seen God like this but for her trouble. She may never have recognized His voice, but for her pain. That's how that desert spring got it's name, from her personal encounter with God, and, that desert spring is still there. That's why she named it, so that any other time she wanders off into the wilderness of life, any other time she is "there" again, she will remember El-Roi. That He is with her, that He hears her, and that He knows every detail of her story. Anytime she is in the wilderness, again, she can remember and be refreshed all over again at that spring in the place called "there". You see, for Hagar, "here" in Genesis 16:8, became "there" in Genesis 16:14. It became a place of remembrance, a memorial, a testimony to God's faithfulness that will refresh and encourage Hagar for the rest of her life. As we'll see later, she found herself in the wilderness again, and this encounter with El Roi was an anchor that helped and sustained her.

Hagar Obeyed God

Hagar obeyed God. She left the desert, went back to her mistress and gave birth to her son, and Abram named him Ishmael. That tells me that Hagar told him her story, of how God met her as a runaway girl, pregnant-out-of-wedlock. You see, the solution was not to kill the baby. Even though her baby was conceived in a sad way, and even though his mother was a slave girl who was used, abused, and dumped, God still had a plan for that baby. He still provided for Hagar and her baby, and He still had a great future for her and her baby. Abortion was not the solution then and it's not the solution now. Psalm 127 says that, children are a gift from the Lord and the fruit of the womb is His reward. Our children belong to God.

Today, we are reading the story of Hagar and being encouraged by it, because she bore that child. And, the story of Hagar, a little slave girl is in the Bible because of that baby that she bore; and today this little, abused, slave girl, is impacting the entire world and human history because of her son, that boy Ishmael that she bore at such great inconvenience and heartache. Ishmael is the ancestor of the Arab nations. You see, a baby changes everything! If you are pregnant today and considering whether or not to kill that baby, I ask you to do what Hagar did. Talk to God about your baby. You don't know the potential of that baby and the future that God has planned for him or her. Don't kill that baby! Go to God and let Him give you a vision of the future of your baby.

I wish this was the end of Hagar's story, and that she, Abram, and Sarai lived happily ever after, but that is not what happened. We pick up her story in Genesis 21. By this time, God had changed the names of Abram and Sarai to Abraham and Sarah, and He has kept His promise, and they had given birth to their son Isaac. Abraham had a huge party to celebrate, and Sarah saw Ishmael making fun of Isaac. So, she turned to Abraham and said to him, "Get rid of that slave woman and her son. He is not going to share the inheritance with my son, Isaac. I won't have it!" This upset Abraham very much because Ishmael was his son. But God told Abraham, "Do not be upset over the boy and your servant. Do whatever Sarah tells you, for Isaac is the son through whom your descendants will be counted. But I will also make a nation of the descendants of Hagar's son because he is your son, too."

Simply stated, what happened to Hagar was unfair! It is sadly, the story of so many young women, who are left stranded with an unwanted pregnancy and abandoned. Here her situation is particularly tragic because these are God's people, who treated her so shamefully. The same Sarah who had given her to Abraham as a surrogate mom, now abandons her and her child, because she had given birth to her own son Isaac. It's not right, it's not fair, and it's not Christian. But sadly, these things happen and Hagar was left holding the bag.

This is why we must be careful the choices we make, and the voices we allow to influence our lives. You cannot allow other people to make choices for your life, who will not take accountability for the consequences of that choice. You must take personal responsibility for your own life and choices. It's not enough that your friend told you to do this, or that you are "in love". When push comes to shove, your decision is your responsibility, and the outcome is your problem. So many young girls have been abandoned with an unwanted pregnancy, because they listened to a young man who convinced them to have sex outside of marriage, and told them how much they loved them, and would be there for them. The sad reality is that once you get pregnant, it's your problem. The young man absconds and you are left to fend for yourself and your baby. Here's the simple solution. If he wants sex, he must put a ring on it!

Sarah was supremely selfish and did not consider Hagar and her son at all. She did not consider Abraham either, after all Ishmael was his son. It's easy for us to tell people to give up things that don't mean anything to us, but means the world to them. Sarah could say, "get rid of that slave woman and her son", because she did not have a connection to Ishmael. She created this big mess and does not care who gets hurt. Notice how her tone and description of Hagar has degenerated. Her original plan was that she, Sarah, would raise Hagar's child as her own. But now that she has given birth to Isaac, Hagar is "that slave woman" and Ishmael is "her son". It is sad, and it is not right, but it is human nature. This is why we cannot put our trust in human beings, no matter whether they are pastors, leaders, or mentors. Abraham and Sarah are God's covenant people, but yet, they made terrible choices that hurt others.

Abraham was grieved by Sarah's demand that he send Ishmael away. Ishmael was his first son. Though he was not the son of promise, he was nonetheless his son. But God told Abraham to go along with Sarah's demand, and promised to take care of Ishmael. Now, that is the promise that you can count on. God will keep His promise. He promised Abraham that He would make Ishmael's descendants into a great nation. Looking at the Arab nations today, we know that God kept His promise.

In obedience to God, Abraham got up early the next morning, prepared food and a container of water, and strapped them on Hagar's shoulders. Then he sent her away with their son. It is unfortunate that Abraham sent Hagar away into the wilderness with only one container of water. We don't know how much food he gave her, but it was small enough to be strapped on her shoulders. With these meager supplies and no destination, the Bible says that she wandered aimlessly in the wilderness of Beersheba.

Stories like this validate the fact that the Bible is indeed the word of God. If human beings wrote the Bible on their own volition, they would not include these glaring failures of Abraham and Sarah. We want our heroes to be super-heroes, gallant, and flawless. Only in the Bible do you find heroes who look like you and me. Men and women who are full of flaws and yet are used by God. Men like David who was an adulterer and murderer, but whom God called a man after His own heart; men like Moses who was a murderer and yet became the revered leader and lawgiver of Israel; men like apostle Paul who was a persecutor and murderer of Christians, who became the great apostle Paul who did more to spread the gospel of Jesus Christ than any other apostle. You see, God uses flawed people, because that is the only kind of people there are.

Sometimes, I run into people who want to pretend that the founding fathers of this nation were perfect men. America is the greatest nation on earth and yes, our founding fathers were great men, men of tremendous leadership, fortitude, and supreme resolve. Men who left an incredible and indelible legacy of a great nation not only for us, but for the whole world. But these men were also slave holders, some of them had sexual relations with their slaves, like Abraham, some of them mistreated their slaves, and some of them were men driven by self-interest, who, like Sarah, used and abused people. And it is okay to talk about it, it's okay to admit it. It does not mean that they were bad men or that their legacy is being tarnished. It is simply the truth, that they are human beings, human beings with failures and flaws, just like any other human being.

El Roi All Over Again!

Hagar wandered aimlessly in the desert with her son until their water ran out. Then she put him in the shade of a bush, and she went and sat down by herself about fifty yards away. She didn't want to watch her son die before her eyes. She and Ishmael began to cry. God heard the boy crying, and the Angel of God called to Hagar from heaven. He said, "Hagar, what's wrong? Do not be afraid! God has heard the boy crying as he lies there. Go to him and comfort him, for I will make a great nation from his descendants." Then God opened Hagar's eyes, and she saw a well full of water. She quickly filled her water container and gave her boy a drink. And God was with Ishmael as he grew up in the wilderness. He became a skillful archer, and settled in the wilderness of Paran.

Once again, God steps in to clean up the mess. He hears the cry of Ishmael, speaks to Hagar, comforts and encourages her, and gives her hope for the future. He reassures her that even though it looks so bleak and overwhelming right now, this is not the end of the story for her and her son, and that He still has a great future planned for Ishmael. Then he provided for them. He opened her eyes to see a well full of water, and she gave her boy a drink.

We have seen this scene before, in Genesis 16, when Hagar was running away from Sarai. She ran right into God. He called her by name and provided for her and her son. Here she is again, back in the desert, and here is God again. Once again, He calls her by name, provides for her, and gives her a vision for her future and the future of her son. Hagar will always remember El-Roi. The God who is with her, hears her, and knows every detail of her story.

You can expect the same. If you are in a wilderness today, be on the lookout for El Roi. Listen for His voice calling your name. If you are worried about your children who are in trouble, or in the wilderness far away from God, listen for the voice of El Roi. He has the blueprint for your future and the future of your children. God's promise is the one promise you can count upon. God will always keep His promise. He promised Hagar that He would make Ishmael's descendants into a great nation and He kept that promise. He will keep His promise to you, no matter what.

CHAPTER 4
Th High Cost of Low Living

LOT

Lot is the nephew of the great patriarch Abraham. We first meet him in Genesis 11. At the end of a long list of the descendants of Shem, the son of Noah, we read that Terah, the father of Abraham took his son, then named Abram, his daughter in law, then named Sarai, and his grand-son Lot and moved away from their hometown, Ur of the Chaldeans, to go to the land of Canaan. Lot's father, Haran, was deceased, and so, his grandfather raised him. As Terah and his family were on their way to Canaan, they came to a town named Haran, the same name as his dead son. Terah stopped in Haran and settled there. Maybe it was unresolved grief over the death of his son that prompted Terah to settle in Haran. The Bible doesn't tell us why. All we know is that he settled in Haran and died there. He did not complete his proposed journey to Canaan. After Terah's death, God spoke to Abram to pick up where his father left off. Terah had unfinished business and God wanted Abram to complete it. The Bible states in Genesis 12:1-3, 5:

"The Lord said to Abram, "Leave your native country, your relatives, and your father's family, and go to the land that I will show you. I will make you into a great nation. I will bless you and make you famous, and you will be a blessing to others. I will bless those who bless you and curse those who curse you. All the families on earth will be blessed through you." So, Abram took his wife, Sarai, his nephew Lot, and all his wealth—and headed for the land of Canaan."

Abram obeyed God and left Haran. He took Lot along with him and they set out on the journey of a lifetime. They arrived in the land of Canaan and settled there. After a while, there was a famine in the land, so, they left Canaan for a brief stay in Egypt, and when the famine was over, they returned back to Canaan. God blessed Abram and Lot, their flocks and herds multiplied, so much so that their herdsmen quarreled over the grazing land for their livestock. They needed more land for grazing. So, Abram said to Lot: "The whole countryside is open to you. Take your choice of any section of the land you want, and we will separate."

Lot took a long look at the fertile plains of the Jordan valley in the direction of Zoar. The whole area was well watered, like the garden of the Lord or the beautiful land of Egypt. (This was before the Lord destroyed Sodom and Gomorrah.) Lot chose for himself the whole Jordan valley to the east. He went there with his flocks and servants and parted company with his uncle Abram. So, Abram settled in the land of Canaan, he moved his camp to Hebron and settled near the oak grove of Mamre. There he built another altar to the Lord.

As this story unfolds, Lot made three critical sets of choices that had tremendous negative outcomes for him and his family.

Lot's First Choice

Abram gave Lot the option to choose first the section of land that he would occupy, and Lot made a choice. He chose the fertile plains of the Jordan valley. That fateful decision ultimately led to the loss of everything that Lot had. It led to the loss of his wife, his wealth, and eventually, the future of his children. Let's examine the factors that drove that choice:

Decision Drivers

1. The first factor that drove Lot's choice is pride and self-interest. Lot put himself first: he chose first. Even though Abram gave him the option of first selection, he could have declined and deferred to his uncle. In the Middle Eastern culture, it was customary to defer to one's elders out of respect, so, it would have been the norm for Lot to defer to Abram and give him first choice, but he did not. Philippians 2:3 states that a mark of humility is putting others first. But Lot did not do that. He chose first.

2. Secondly, he chose by what he saw with his natural eyes: The Bible says that he took a long look and chose based on what he saw. The land looked so good! It was

fertile, lush and green. The whole area was well watered, like the garden of the Lord or the beautiful land of Egypt. All Lot saw, was sweet, green, grass and rich vegetation as far as the eye could see, and in his mind's eye, he saw all the fat, healthy, and robust livestock he would raise on this land. He was going to be rich! So, he chose based on natural sight and expectation of financial gain. This is exactly what the Bible tells us not to do. Second Corinthians 5:7 tells us to walk by faith and not by sight.

3. Thirdly, Lot chose the path of least resistance. He chose the plains. There were no hills to climb, and no hard labor; only easy, breezy, green, plains. The Jordan river provided an abundant water source, and with no hill country, this looked to Lot like easy street.

4. Fourthly, Lot chose selfishly. His choice did not include any consideration for Abram. The Bible says that he chose "for himself" the whole Jordan valley. He did not think of sharing a portion of that lush grazing land with his uncle's livestock. He chose the whole valley for himself, and his uncle had to move to the hill country.

5. Fifthly, Lot chose from experience. The land looked familiar, it was like the garden of the Lord or the beautiful land of Egypt. Lot and his uncle had just come back from Egypt. They had gone there to escape the famine in the land of Canaan. While they were there, their livestock grew and multiplied. So, when his uncle gave him the first choice, Lot looked at the Jordan valley, and it looked

just like the lush land of Egypt, and he fell for the trap. Like Lot, the devil has trapped so many people with things and places that look familiar. In fact, there are demon spirits who specialize in this type of assignment. They are called "familiar spirits". So, beware of the snare of the familiar.

6. Sixthly, and most significantly, we never read of Lot ever building an altar to the Lord in the valley, or of God ever speaking to him. An altar is a time and/or place that is sanctified or set apart for God. It is a time and/or place where you meet with God. In Exodus 20:23-24, God said to the Children of Israel, "Remember, you must not make any idols of silver or gold to rival me. Build for me an altar made of earth. Build my altar wherever I cause my name to be remembered, and I will come to you and bless you." An altar is a declaration of dependence on God, and an acknowledgment of His ownership and Lordship over your life. It cultivates the presence of God, and an ability to hear and recognize His voice. Abram raised several altars to the Lord. As soon as he moved to Hebron, he built an altar there and sought the Lord. We never read of Lot raising even one altar to the Lord.

The "Buts"- The Critical Intersection Points

Have you ever had a situation where you needed to make a decision about something or someone, and everything looked great on the outside, but you had a hesitation in your spirit? It's like someone threw a red flag! Somehow, you feel that something is not quite right, but you can't put your finger on exactly what it is. You have a nagging suspicion that things are not what they appear to be and that there is more than meets the eye. Whenever that happens, you have come to a "But". These are the critical intersection points that you and I often come to in our decision-making process.

This has happened to me personally several times. One time, as a single woman, I met a nice guy at a conference. He was a Christian and loved the Lord. We studied the Bible together, and had a lot in common professionally. He was convinced that I was "The One" for him, and I liked him too, but every time he asked me to move our friendship forward into a dating relationship, an alarm bell would go off in my spirit. Something wasn't quite right, but I couldn't put my finger on it. It was very frustrating! Everything looked great on the outside, but every time I tried to step forward with him, I had a check in my spirit. Finally, I decided to walk away. Later, I found out that he had been living a double life and had major, secret, addictions that eventually wrecked his life and career. This is why you have to pay attention to Holy Spirit and His "Buts".

In making his choice to move to Sodom, Lot came to two "Buts". These are small parenthetical inserts in the text that highlight red flags that Lot missed entirely. He was so focused on what he saw with his natural eyes that he did not look with his spiritual eyes or pay attention to the inner voice warning him of these "Buts".

The first "But" is a small historical parenthetical about the land. The Bible said in verse 10 that the land looked lush and fertile: (But this was before the Lord destroyed Sodom and Gomorrah.) Even though the land looked lush and green on the outside, it would soon be destroyed. This "But" represents the transient benefits that the devil uses to lure folks into making permanent bad decisions. So many people have made permanent, life altering, decisions to meet a temporary need. Many people are in prison today because they made a reckless choice to address a short-term problem without thinking through the long term consequences. In the Bible, Esau sold his birthright, an extremely valuable inheritance right, for a bowl of lentil soup. In Hebrews 12:16-17, the Bible warns us to "Be careful that no one among you is immoral or godless, becoming careless about God's blessings, like Esau who traded away his rights as the firstborn for a simple meal. And we know that later on when he wanted to inherit his father's blessing, he was turned away, even though he begged for it with bitter tears, for it was too late then to repent." Today, the world, the devil, the flesh, and the marketers have one goal, to push you and I to make permanent, expensive, decisions to address temporary needs. We must say no!

The second "But" was about the people. The Bible said, in verse 13, that the people of Sodom were extremely wicked and constantly sinned against the Lord. Shakespeare said in Macbeth, that "there's no art to find the mind's construction in the face." God said it a lot simpler. In Jeremiah 17:9, God said that the heart of mankind is deceitful and desperately wicked. You cannot discern the heart by looking at the face. God has to guide your decision making when it comes to people, because He alone knows the heart. John 2:24, states that Jesus did not entrust Himself to people because He knew all about people and did not commit Himself to them.

When it comes to human hearts, we need God's help to determine our choices. The good news is that God promises to help us. In

Psalm 32, He says, "I will guide you along the best pathway for your life. I will stay close to you, instructing and guiding you along. I will advise you and watch over you with my eyes as your guide. So, don't make it difficult; don't be stubborn when I take you where you've not been before. Don't make me tug you and pull you along. Just come with me to the great future I have planned for you!" Our response should be "Yes Lord; help me, Lord, to choose right."

Lot couldn't see the "Buts". They were not visible to the naked eye. You need God's help to see them. When we look with our natural eyes, we have sight, but when we seek God, we gain insight because God sees the end from the beginning, and can show us the invisible. This is what we can miss when we rush headlong into decisions and don't stop to pray and ask for God's direction, or when we override His warning signs and move forward over the objections of the Holy Spirit. We need to have discernment and the wisdom of God to see and navigate these critical intersection points.

Do You See What I See?

What we see with our natural eyes are so unreliable, and yet for most people, it's the only reality they know. Hebrews 11:3 tells us that everything that is visible was created from the invisible. This makes clear that the invisible world is the parent of the physical world. Yet, unfortunately, many Christians reverse the order.

While our eyes are a blessing from God and a gift to enable us to interact with this natural world, it can be severely limiting when we use it to measure spiritual truth. This is why the Bible tells us not to walk by sight. First because the devil is such a good liar that he will fabricate evidence to back up his lies. If what you see is what you believe, the devil will work to make sure that you see plenty of lies. In Genesis 37, Joseph's brothers, soaked his coat of many colors in goat's blood and presented that false evidence to their father, and he, of his own accord, jumped to the conclusion that a wild beast had devoured Joseph, even though that was not the truth and his brothers did not actually say so. Jacob merely believed what he saw with his eyes and came to his own wrong conclusion that Joseph was killed by a wild beast. That conclusion was based on the "evidence of his eyes" but it was fabricated evidence, because the devil will fabricate real evidence to support his lies.

Another reason why we cannot rely on our natural eyes for spiritual insight is that, even when we are seeing actual facts correctly, we can wrongly interpret what we see. In the book of Esther, Haman interpreted the fact that queen Esther invited him alone to dine with the king, as evidence of his elite status, distinction, and promotion. That was the evidence of his eyes and the interpretation of his mind. But he was dead wrong! Little did he know that Esther's "special" dinner invitation was actually a death sentence.

This is why it is of critical importance that we rely on the Holy Spirit to guide our perception, understanding, and interpretation of what we see. We must pass what we see with our natural eyes through the prism of the word of God and the real time vetting and guidance of the Holy Spirit, to gain spiritual insight, direction, and clarity. That is the only way to make sure that we see what He sees.

Outcomes of Lot's First Choice

Lot's first choice to move his tents near Sodom and settle there had terrible outcomes:

1. Sodom was not at all what it looked like. It had looked like the garden of Eden, but in reality, it was Satan occupied territory. It was the headquarters of sin, immorality, and depravity.

2. Soon after Lot settled there, Sodom was attacked by a coalition of four kings. Lot and his family were taken into captivity, and the livestock and dream of wealth that drove him to choose Sodom were all lost. The Bible says that the invaders "captured Lot—and carried off everything he owned." Sadly, what happened to Lot is what happens to many Christians. When we fail to consult God or wait for His timing, we can make choices that are driven by sight, our appetites, or ungodly ambition, and end up losing everything. That is what happened to Lot. His first choice to settle in Sodom landed him in captivity and Abram had to go to war with the invaders to rescue him and his household.

   You may be in that place right now, where you, like Abram, is being called upon to go and rescue a friend, spouse, child, or family member who made a wrong choice, and was taken captive by the devil. Don't despair! God has a promise for you in Isaiah 49:24-26: He says, "Can the prey be taken from a mighty man, or the captives of a tyrant be delivered? For this is what the Lord says: "Even the captives of a mighty man will be taken, and the prey of a tyrant will be delivered; I will contend with the one who contends with you, and I will save your children." It doesn't matter what the devil, people, or your circumstances say, God's voice overrules, and He says that the captives will be delivered. So, be encouraged. The Lord has already given you victory! The devil will not win in the lives of your children.

3. For Lot, there's more! Genesis 14:10 tells us that hidden in the plains of Sodom were tar or asphalt pits. Pits that ensnared and trapped people who tried to get away. You don't see these pits at first, but if you try to escape from Sodom, you will fall into these slimy pits. Hebrews 12 warns us about the sin that can so easily ensnare and trip us up.

   How many people in our churches are trapped, right now, by the tar pits of Sodom; places and things that promised them enjoyment, relief, and comfort, but which eventually became shackles, yokes of bondage, and chains that bound them, and now holds them captive. The websites that they went to for fun, relief, and entertainment, but which has ended up destroying their lives and the relationships that are important to them. These are the tar pits of Sodom.

4. Anyone who managed to escape Sodom, had to flee to the mountains for safety. There was no other option. The sad irony is that safety is found only in the mountains, the same mountains that Lot has tried so hard to avoid. In Psalm 121, David said, I lift up my eyes to the hills, from where comes my help? My help comes from the Lord, the maker of heaven and earth. We must be willing to go up to the mountains with God and to meet with God. He alone is our source, helper,

refuge. and defender. If we seek God in the mountains, He will hide us in the cleft of the rock, until the danger passes.

Lot's Second Choice:

Genesis 18 records that, the sin of Sodom was a stench in God's nostrils. Sodom was so corrupt that the only solution was total annihilation by fire. Abraham interceded for Sodom. He pleaded with God for the life of Lot, his family, and the people of Sodom. Abraham said to God, what if there are fifty righteous people in Sodom, you couldn't possibly destroy them along with the wicked? God promised to spare Sodom if there were fifty righteous people in it. Abraham didn't stop there. He pleaded and negotiated with God all the way down to ten people, and God promised not to destroy Sodom if there were ten righteous people in it. I think Abraham stopped at ten because he truly believed that a city the size of Sodom will surely have at least ten righteous people in it, particularly as his nephew Lot lived there.

Abraham probably thought that Lot, his family, and the servants and herdsmen who moved to Sodom with him were at least ten people. Besides, all these years that he had lived in Sodom, surely, Lot must have turned some of the people over to Jehovah. But sadly, that was not the case. Not only did Lot not gain any new converts in Sodom, he lost to Sodom, many souls that moved in there with him.

Genesis 19 tells the story: That evening two angels came to the entrance of the city of Sodom. Lot was sitting there, and when he saw them, he welcomed them and invited them to his home, where he prepared a feast for them, and they ate. Before they went to bed, the men of Sodom, both young and old, the whole population, surrounded the house. They called out to Lot and said, "Where are the men who came to you tonight? Send them out to us so we can have sex with them!" Lot went outside and begged them not to do this evil. Then he said, Look, I've got two virgin daughters. I'll bring them out to you, and you can do whatever you want to them. However, don't do anything to these men, because they have come under the protection of my roof." The men of Sodom said to him, "Get out of the way!" "This one came here as an alien, but he's acting like a judge! Now we'll do more harm to you than to them." At this point, the angels pulled Lot inside the house and struck the men of Sodom with blindness so they could not find the door to come in.

What we see here is the high cost of low living; the tragic result of a reprobate society that rejects God, and the failure of a Christian church that has lost its voice and witness. It is clear that:

1. Lot was righteous. He approached the angels the same way that Abraham did, and he was hospitable and generous, like Abraham was. It is clear that Lot still practiced the godly values and principles that Abraham taught him. Sodom had not taken that away from him.

2. He did not approve of the behavior and lifestyle of the people of Sodom. He knew it was wrong, and called it evil. But he stopped short of telling them that it was an evil against God. Lot had become "politically correct". He did not tell them that homosexuality was a sin against God. He did not want to offend them. So, he said, "don't do anything to these men, because they have come under the protection of my roof".

Contrast that with Joseph who when faced with sexual sin in Egypt called it a "great wickedness and sin against God".

3. Lot's daughters were still virgins, which is a great testament to Lot's righteousness. Being able to raise his daughters as virgins in a culture as depraved and corrupt as Sodom, is quite a feat and speaks volumes about Lot's personal and private devotion to Yahweh. However, the fact that all the men of Sodom, the whole population, came out for the homosexual orgy showed the sad fact that Lot had not been effective as a witness for Jehovah. He had not won anybody over to God. In fact, he had lost many souls to Sodom. In Genesis 13, we read that Lot moved to Sodom with his servants and herdsmen. Now, they are not on his side. They are part of the crowd wanting homosexual sex. Also, this means that even the young men who were engaged to marry his daughters, his future sons in law, were as depraved as the rest of the men of Sodom. They were in that crowd too!

4. From their response, it is clear that the men of Sodom were not used to having Lot witness to them or tell them about the ways of Jehovah. They did not have any qualms whatsoever, about coming to his house and demanding that he bring out his guests for homosexual sex. The brazenness of their approach indicates that this behavior is common and their response when he tried to stop them, showed that they were not used to hearing much of any protests from Lot. They said to him, "Get out of the way!" adding, "This one came here as an alien, but he's acting like a judge! Then they threatened to harm him.

This may be why Lot had not spoken up previously. Fear! Fear of these people and their persecution. Fear that he may be hurt or in today's culture, "canceled" by them, had made him keep his mouth shut. But on this day, Lot learned the lesson that we in America must learn. You cannot compromise your way to victory. You cannot rebuke the devil you are walking with. A Christian church that goes along to get along, a church that silences its voice out of fear, will see the destruction not only of itself, but of the nation. Like Martin Luther King Jr. said, "to ignore evil is to be accomplice to it".

5. Lot's story illustrates the tragedy of being an undercover Christian. People who think that as long as I am a Christian in my own home, that is enough. I don't need to get involved in what other people do. Religion is a private matter and how people serve their God is their business. Well, Lot thought so too, until the men of Sodom told him to send his house guests outside to be sexually molested. I guess they believed that as long as they did not molest them inside Lot's house, that Lot would be okay with it. This is the same situational ethics and relative morality that is drowning our modern society in a cesspool of evil. We live in a time when there are no moral absolutes, no right or wrong, good or bad. But God does have a standard and we, as the church, must be willing to stand up and speak up for biblical truth.

Because of Lot's complacency, Sodom lost, not only all its men, but the future generation as well. The Bible says that the whole male population turned out for the homosexual orgy, including the young. This is why Sodom had to be destroyed. The children were lost and corrupted as well. You see, by the time Lot finally decided to go outside his house to witness to the people of Sodom, and to speak out against the sin of Sodom, it was too late.

This reminds me of the story of Martin Niemöller. He was a cadet in the German Navy and commander of a U boat in World War 1. In 1920, he decided to follow the path of his father and went to seminary to become a pastor. When Hitler rose to power, Niemöller enthusiastically welcomed him and the Third Reich. But later, he came to see Hitler as a dictator, and publicly opposed him. As a result, he spent the last seven years of Nazi rule in concentration camps. Later, Pastor Niemöller described his attitude to the Nazis in a sobering quote:

First, they came for the socialists, and I did not speak out because I was not a socialist.
Then they came for those in the trade unions, and I did not speak out, because I was not in a trade union.
Then they came for the Jews, and I did not speak out because I was not a Jew.
Then they came for me, and by this time, there was no one left to speak out for me.

This is what happened to Lot. He had waited too long to speak up. Second Peter 2:8 clearly tells us that Lot was a righteous man and that his righteous soul was vexed by the depravity of Sodom, but it does not tell us that he spoke out against it. He went along, to get along, and in so doing, lost his credibility and impact. He became like that salt Jesus described in Matthew 5:13, that lost its saltiness, and is therefore worthless and good for nothing. In trying to play it safe and avoid offending the people of Sodom, Lot lost his witness. We also know that he did not build an altar to God in Sodom. I believe that those two are connected.

6. Lot paid a terrible price for his silence. He had lived so long in Sodom and silently put up with so much evil that it warped his thinking. The erosion in his thinking is evident in the fact that he offered his virgin daughters to be raped. Lot had lost touch with Jehovah and his word, and so his moral compass was faulty, so faulty, that he thought that he could solve one depravity with another. His flawed thought process was that homosexuality was evil, but rape was okay. It is so sad, when a man or woman of God compromises to such an extent that they no longer know what is good and bad, right and wrong. They begin to choose between levels of bad, and say things like: "At least, this is not as bad as that."

It's the same thing we see in today's world where the devil will offer, and some Christians accept to swap one type of bondage for another. For example, stop smoking weed, but abuse alcohol. This is the hallmark of Christians who have lived so close to the edge of sin and iniquity, that they can't tell which way is up. They have lost their way and their identity as sons and daughters of God. We see this same double standard in Christians who judge others because they sin differently than they do. For these Christians, homosexuality is a grave sin, but pre-marital sex is okay, or, abortion is a mortal sin, but racism and racists killing a black person is okay. This shows how far they have drifted from God's word and standard.

7. The men of Sodom pulled out their trump card, which is the mantra of every wayward generation. They said to Lot, "Don't judge us!" I have heard that for most of its history, the most popular Bible verse in America was John 3:16. Both Christians and non-Christians alike know that verse. However, it is my understanding that in recent years, another verse has overtaken John 3:16 in popularity. That verse is Matthew 7:1, which says, "Do not judge so that you will not be judged." This is the gag order of a godless generation on the church. It is the devil's weapon of choice to beat down the church, drown the voice of Christians, and stop us from fulfilling our God given mandate to be salt and light in the world. Our response must be an emphatic "No!"

The Verdict is in, Sodom Must Go!

The brazen display of godlessness and flagrant immorality by the men of Sodom, sealed the fate of their city. The heavenly investigation was complete and the verdict was passed. Sodom must be destroyed. There was no other way. So, the angels turned their attention to saving Lot and his family.

"They said to Lot, "Do you have anyone else here: a son-in-law, your sons and daughters, or anyone else in the city who belongs to you? Get them out of this place, because we are about to destroy this city. So, Lot went out and spoke to his sons-in-law, the young men who were going to marry his daughters. "Get up," he said. "Get out of this place, for the Lord is about to destroy the city!" But his sons-in-law thought he was joking." (Genesis 19:12).

How tragic! Lot was not even a credible witness to his future sons in law. This is not surprising, given that they were part of the crowd the previous evening. Also, the fact that they thought that his grave warning to escape destruction in Sodom was only a joke, tells me that Lot's sons-in-law did not know Yahweh. Lot's daughters were engaged to marry men who did not know or serve God, and all this happened because Lot, a righteous man, chose to live in Sodom for wealth, financial gain, and ease. From heaven's perspective, he had nothing to show for all the years he lived in Sodom. He had left no impact, no converts, no footprints, and no legacy.

The next morning the situation became urgent. The angels said to Lot, "Hurry, take your wife and your two daughters who are here. Get out right now, or you will be swept away in the destruction of the city!" When Lot still hesitated, the angels grabbed him, his wife and two daughters and rushed them to safety outside the city.

Lot literally escaped Sodom only with the shirt on his back. I believe that he hesitated to leave Sodom because it dawned on him, at that moment, that he was leaving all his material wealth inside Sodom. All the livestock and wealth that led him to Sodom in the first place, were all going to be destroyed. It's the same thing with us. The Bible says that everything we see on earth will one day be burnt up by fire – all the wealth, fame, position, and possessions in this world, will one day go up in flames, and sadly, some Christians will be like Lot. They would lose everything because they did not lay their treasure up in heaven. First Corinthians 3 tells us plainly that we can build our lives with gold, silver, and precious stones, or with wood, hay, and straw. Each person's work will be put through the fire to test its quality. "If the work stands the test of fire, the person will be rewarded. If the work is consumed by the fire, that person will suffer great loss. Yet he himself will barely escape destruction, like someone rescued out of a burning house." This is what happened to Lot. The fire burnt all his possessions, and took his wife also. Make no mistake, lives built with hay, wood, and straw will burn up and those people, like Lot, will suffer tragic loss.

You see, only two things are eternal, the word of God and the souls of men. If you are not invested in those two things, you will not have any treasure up in heaven, and everything else you invest in on planet earth will one day be burnt up!

Lot Chooses Zoar

When Lot and his family were safely outside Sodom, one of the angels told them to, "Run for their lives! And don't look back or stop anywhere in the valley! Escape to the mountains, or you will be swept away!" But Lot protested; "Oh no, my Lord!" he begged. "You have been so gracious to me, saved my life, and shown me great kindness. But I cannot go to the mountains. Disaster would catch up to me there, and I would soon die. See, there is a small village nearby. Please let me go there instead; don't you see how small it is? Then my life will be saved." "All right," the angel said, "I will grant your request. I will not destroy the little village. But hurry! Escape there, for I can do nothing until you arrive there."

Here again, we see Lot make another disastrous choice. Even though he lost everything in Sodom, he still had the same mindset that landed him in Sodom in the first place. The angels specifically told him to escape to the mountains, but he would not. Lot loved the valley. He was told not to stop anywhere in the valley, but that is exactly what he wanted and insisted on doing. Lot was so used to low living that he would not make the effort to come up higher, even when God specifically directed him to.

Decision Drivers

What were the drivers of Lot's decision to go to Zoar?

1. Once again, Lot chose by what he saw with his natural eyes, over the word of God. He said to the angel, "see, there is a small village nearby, let me go there instead".

2. He chose based on ease and convenience. The village was nearby, and it was in the valley. So, he didn't have far to go, and there was no hard labor required.

3. Lot chose selfishly. He chose based on self-interest. His only focus was to save his own life. He didn't consider his daughters and their future.

4. Lot chose from experience. The land was familiar. It was right there in the valley, in the plains of Sodom. The angels would have destroyed Zoar and all the cities in the valley because they were not much different from Sodom. But Lot would not let them. He requested permission to go to Zoar, when the angels specifically told him to get away from it! So, the angels granted his request and did not destroy Zoar, but as we will soon

see, that was another bad choice. That is probably one prayer that Lot later wished was not answered.

5. Fear is the biggest driver of all of Lot's choices. Every time he made a decision, there was an undercurrent of fear: 1) He moved to Sodom due to fear of lack or financial failure, 2) he did not speak out against the sin of Sodom due to fear of persecution, 3) When Sodom was destroyed, he decided to escape to Zoar due to fear of death, and later, 4) he ran away from Zoar due to fear of the people. Fear is bondage. It opens the door to the devil and attracts the very thing that you fear.

Fear is a spirit and it ruined Lot's life. Today, our world is riddled with fear, but God has not given us the spirit of fear, but of power, love, and a sound mind. So, we must say "No" to fear. How do we do that? Through prayer. Philippians 4:6 says, "Don't worry about anything; instead, pray about everything. Tell God what you need, and thank him for all he has done. Then you will experience God's peace." When we pray, we cast our cares on the Lord and exchange our fears for His peace. This is why Lot made so many bad choices. He did not pray. Unlike Abraham, he never raised one altar to the Lord. If you are struggling with fear, worry, and anxiety. I encourage you to turn your worries over to God in prayer and receive His peace and help today.

Results of the Choice

Lot lost everything! He even lost his wife. The pull of Sodom was too great for her. So, she disobeyed the angels, looked back, and was turned into a pillar of salt. That pillar stood as a monument to Lot's failure. His failure to be salt and light to the people of Sodom.

Lot's Third Choice

The saga continues! Genesis 19:30, states that, "Afterward Lot left Zoar because he was afraid of the people there, and he went to live in a cave in the mountains with his two daughters."

Remember that the angels had told Lot not to go to Zoar, because it was not very different from Sodom. In fact, the Bible tells us that Zoar was aligned with Sodom. In Genesis 14:2, we see that the king of Zoar marched out with and fought alongside the king of Sodom. They were in league together. So, the angels would have destroyed Zoar along with Sodom, except that Lot asked to go there. Now his choice, made in self-will, fear, and self-interest has back fired. He found out what the angels knew all along, that Zoar was no good. He could have trusted the word and voice of God, and believed that God knew what was best for him, but he had to do it his own way, and find out for himself, the hard way.

On that note, let's take a praise break and thank God for all the prayers He did not answer in our own lives. Thank God for that crazy man or woman you wanted to marry, but God said "No"; that job you thought was perfect for you, but which would have ended up drawing you away from God; the times when you wanted things that God knew would destroy you and he said "No". Thank God for the times He wrecked your plans when He saw that your plans were about to wreck you. Thank God for protecting you from what you thought you wanted and blessing you with what you didn't even know that you needed! Thank you, Lord!

Lot's self-will and sight driven decisions have landed him in Zoar. But now, he's in trouble. He can't stay in Zoar. So, he fled to the mountains in fear. He did not stop to seek God for direction, or to consider the life and future of his daughters, how will they survive in isolation, living alone in the mountains? Who will they marry? Never once in his decision making process did Lot seek God, ask the Lord for guidance, or allow God to enter his decision making framework. It was all about him. The sad irony is that he eventually ended up running to the mountains. The same mountains he avoided the first time that Abram gave him a choice, and the second time when the angels specifically told him to run to the mountains. Both times, he would have gone to the mountains with God's favor, blessing, and protection. But he refused. Now, he eventually ended up in the mountains, but by this time, it was too late. He was on his own.

It is unclear why Lot did not join up with his uncle Abraham in the mountains. Maybe pride and shame kept him away. He did not want to look like a failure, or maybe he was too embarrassed to ask for help. His uncle had bailed him out once before when he and his family were captured as prisoners of war. Maybe Lot was too embarrassed to ask for help again, or maybe he was afraid that he was a disappointment to Abraham, or that he was penniless and did not want to be a burden to his uncle. It's unclear why he did not reach out to Abraham, but it was a missed opportunity to redeem himself and his family. Maybe if he had reached out to his uncle, he would have salvaged some of the ashes of his life. But instead, he fled to a cave, in the mountains, alone.

This is a common pattern in the lives of people who are running away from God, or the authority figures that God has placed in their lives, like children who rebel against their parents and run away from home. Unfortunately, when things don't turn out as they expected, the devil uses guilt, condemnation, embarrassment, and shame to keep them from going back home. If that is you today, please hear the voice of God: It's time to go home! It's time to set aside your pride, it's time to say "I'm sorry". Maybe, you walked away from God and went down a path of your own choosing. It's not too late to go home. Your heavenly Father is waiting with arms open wide to receive you and welcome you back home!

Well, unfortunately for Lot, he did not run to God or go back to Abraham. Rather, he ran to hide in a cave in the mountains, and sadly, he began to do what many people do to deal with their shame and guilt. He began to drink. Instead of turning to the Lord for help, he turned to alcohol to numb his pain. The devil told him the lie that he tells many people today, the lie that there is help for them outside of God; that alcohol, weed, porn, and any other "cave" can be a solution. But that is not the truth. Alcohol, weed, pornography, and every other cave you run into to hide is not a viable pathway to freedom. It is yet another type of bondage that will strangle and destroy you, and your family. Turn to God. He is your only real help!

Needless to say, alcohol did not help Lot, not one bit! It made matters worse! In the next scene of this tragic drama, we see the pass-down of Lot's fear and sight based decision making to his children, and alcohol played a starring role. The Bible says that: "One day Lot's older daughter said to her sister, "There are no men left anywhere in this entire area, so we can't get married like everyone else. And our father will soon be too old to have children. Come, let's get him drunk with wine, and then we will have sex with him. That way we will preserve our family line through our father." (Genesis 19:31-32).

Lot's daughter did exactly what she had seen her father do again and again. She looked around with her natural eyes, did not see any other man, and decided that her only option was the sinful choice of incest. She did not pray or seek the Lord for help and direction.

Did you notice how many times the pronoun "we" appeared in that verse of scripture? These girls never once referenced God in their thought process. Remember that they had been engaged to marry men from Sodom, men who were as depraved as the rest of the city, and men who were so insensitive to the voice of God, that they heard His call to escape from Sodom, but did not recognize it. It's like Lot's daughters were raised to marry just about any man. For them, any man will do, even if that man was their father! Contrast that with Abraham, who when it came time for Isaac to be married, refused to let him marry a Canaanite woman, but rather, chose to go back to his own family, to take a wife for Isaac. Lot's daughters did not have that frame of reference. So, since their concept of marriage was to marry any man, when they looked with their natural eyes and the only man around was their father, they resorted to sinful, shameful, incest to get a man. Lot had succeeded in raising his two daughters to be virgins even in Sodom, but he had not taught them that God had a plan for their lives and future, so they ended up committing an abomination, incest with their father, just to get a man. Can you imagine Lot's shame and grief when several months later, he saw his daughters pregnant, and realized what happened?

This is a cautionary tale for singles. If you are a single Christian man or woman, who have been waiting for God and it appears nothing is happening for you in the relationship arena, and now the devil is tempting you to date a non-believer, or to make a sinful choice, or to stay in an ungodly relationship just so you can be with somebody, don't do it! This story about Lot's daughters is a warning for you. Trust God and wait for Him. He works on behalf of those who wait for Him. He is the way maker, miracle worker, and promise keeper. He will perfect all that concerns you. Do not believe the devil's lie that you will die single and alone. God sees you and has a plan for your future. Lot's daughters gave birth to sons, and called them Moab and Ammon. Throughout ancient history, those boys and their descendants were enemies of the people of Israel.

Abraham Vs Lot

Why is it that Abraham succeeded and Lot failed? What made the difference? Let's compare their decision making processes:

1. Lot repeatedly chose by what he saw with his natural eyes, while Abraham chose based on his relationship with God and God's voice and direction.

2. Abraham was obedient to God, but Lot was not. In Genesis 12:1, God said to Abram, "go from your land, and your family, to the land I will show you" and Abram went. He did not argue, question, or doubt. He simply

obeyed. Lot on the other hand was specifically told by the angels to escape to the mountains for safety and he did not. He said, "Disaster would befall me there, and I would soon die." Clearly, it's either he did not believe the angels or thought he knew better. Keep in mind that Abram heard the voice of God in his heart and obeyed. Lot on the other hand, had Angels in human form who told him to escape to the mountains for safety and he did not, and this is after he had confirmed that these were Angels because they struck all the men of Sodom with blindness. The lesson is clear, obedience is the only way to walk with God. Jesus said, if you love me, obey me!

3. Lot chose for wealth and financial gain, but Abram did not. He refused to be seduced by the wealth of Sodom. In Genesis 14, when a coalition of four kings invaded Sodom and took Lot and his family captive, Abram went and fought to get them back. When he came back, the king of Sodom met him and offered him all the recovered plunder, but he turned it down, even though he earned it. After all, he had fought and conquered those invaders, yet he said "No" to the plunder. Money was not his motivation. God and people were his focus. He wanted to recover the souls.

The first thing he did was to give a tithe of all the recovered loot to Melchizedek, a priest of God. By giving the tithe to God, he acknowledged His Lordship and victory in the battle, and he was blessed by Melchizedek. When the king of Sodom offered him the rest of the plunder, he refused and said: "I have raised my hand in an oath to the Lord, God Most High, creator of heaven and earth, that I will not take a thread or sandal strap or anything that belongs to you, so you can never say, I made Abram rich." He knew that God was his source and he would not be tainted with or corrupted by the sinful wealth of Sodom. The blessing he received from Melchizedek was enough. It was all he needed.

Ironically, the king of Sodom was also interested in the souls of people! He offered Abram all the money and possessions, as long as he gets all the souls. It's just like the devil. He will offer you anything on earth, if you will sell your soul to him. The Bible says in Revelation 18:13, that the devil is engaged daily in the buying and selling of human souls. This is why Jesus asked the sobering question in Mark 8:36, "What will it profit a person if he gains the whole world and loses his own soul?" Your soul is of tremendous worth and value. Jesus valued your soul so much that he died to save you. Do not sell your soul to the devil for money, fame, or anything in the world. The devil tried to get Jesus to worship him for money and failed. Jesus said "No", and you can too. In 2 Timothy 6, apostle Paul warns us to watch out for the devil's schemes, because it has crept into the church. It's the mindset that equates money with godliness. The flawed thought process that says, "if I am materially blessed, then God must be happy with my lifestyle". He warns us to reject that lie and those who peddle it.

4. Lot chose based on ease, convenience, experience and familiarity. Both Sodom and Zoar were nearby cities, looked familiar, and were in the valley. He didn't have far to go, and there was no hard labor involved. Abram on the other hand chose based on the voice of God and the pursuit of peace. God said, leave your country to the land that I will show you, and he left without seeing the land. He knew that he was blessed because God said so. God was his source of blessing, and so, no matter where he went, and whatever he did, he would be blessed. His blessing came from God and not his physical address. Abram did not chase the blessing, he ran after God, and the blessing ran after him.

5. Lot chose selfishly. He chose based on self-interest. His only focus was to save his own life. He didn't consider the future of his daughters. Abram chose unselfishly. He considered Lot and gave him first choice of the land, and when Lot was captured, he risked his own life to fight and get him back. Also, Abraham interceded for Lot and his family to deliver them from destruction in Sodom.

6. Fear was a major driver of Lot's choices. Every time he made a decision, there was an undercurrent of fear - fear of failure, fear of persecution, fear of people, fear of death, and so on. Abram had fear as well. In Genesis 12:11-13, when he was going into Egypt, he made a fear based choice to lie about his wife, and he made her lie for him as well. But, unlike Lot, Abram also heard and

obeyed the voice and word of God, and that overrode the voice and power of fear in his life.

7. Lot did not pray or seek God. He never raised a single altar to God. Abram on the other hand, raised altars to God and prayed everywhere he went.

8. Lot was silent about his relationship with Jehovah. He did not tell the men of Sodom about his God, but Abram was the exact opposite. In his very first encounter with the king of Sodom, he told him of his devotion to God. He was bold in his witness, and by so doing, Abram set himself apart from the sin of Sodom. He was clear who he was, and whose he was. He belonged to God and did not want anything to do with Sodom.

9. Abraham acknowledged God as his source: He paid tithe to Melchizedek. We never see any instance of Lot giving to God. Also, honoring God with his tithe brought Abram a blessing from Melchizedek. Hebrews 7:3 tells us that Melchizedek was a type of Christ. So, Abram's choices continued to grow and multiply his influence and blessing; while Lot's choices shrunk his world and brought him destruction and devastation.

10. Lot was blessed as long as he stayed with Abram, but when he struck out on his own, and chose not to do the things that Abram did to attract and maintain the blessing of God, his life fell apart. It is very important that we surround ourselves with godly people, and stay

connected to people who draw us closer to God. If you do that, you will be blessed. But the reverse is also true. If you surround yourself with ungodly people, you will be destroyed along with them. Lot started out pitching his tent near Sodom. He thought he could live near to Sodom, get the financial benefits, and not be influenced by the sin of Sodom. After all, he was not living inside Sodom, just near to it. In Genesis 13:12 we read that Lot set up his tent near Sodom. But by the time we come to Genesis 14:12, he was now living inside Sodom. This is the tragic tale of Christians who flirt with sin. Christians who want to get as close to the line as possible. They don't want to cross the line, but they are comfortable living on the edge. If that is you, Lot's story is a wakeup call for you today! If you continue to live near Sodom, you will eventually end up inside Sodom; little by little, one compromise at a time. Sodom has only one goal, to pull you away from God.

One of the saddest stories in the Bible is the story of King Joash in 2 Kings 11 and 12. He was rescued as a baby and hid in the temple of God by Jehoiada the priest from infancy, to avoid being killed by an evil queen. When he was 7 years old, Jehoiada the priest and the entire nation crowned him king. King Joash flourished and honored God during the lifetime of the priest Jehoiada, his mentor. Second Kings 12:2 says that "Throughout the time the priest Jehoiada instructed him, Joash did what was right in the LORD'S sight". But after Jehoiada died, Joash began to listen to ungodly advice. God send prophets to warn him, but he would not listen. He had not taken the time, while Jehoiada was alive, to build his own personal relationship with God. So, after the priest died, king Joash ended up, not only walking away from God, but also killing the son of Jehoiada the priest, his mentor, because he had brought God's word of correction to him. How tragic!

This is what happened to Lot, he was righteous by association with Abram. He was good as long as he stayed with Abram. He had watched Abram build altars to God and pray, but he never learned to build an altar to God by himself, he never learned to seek God for himself. So, when he separated from Abram, he did not have a personal foundation with God strong enough to maintain ongoing, personal, fellowship and that led to his downfall.

If you are a young person riding on the religious coat tails of your parents, or a Christian living vicariously through your pastor, mentors, or other leaders, you are in dangerous territory. You must learn to dig your own spiritual wells! Seek and know God for yourself, because a second hand relationship with God will never be enough when you are faced with life's challenges.

AFTERWORD

We live in an age of choices, ranging from the mundane, but exhausting choices between a multitude of breakfast cereal options at the grocery store, to life altering choices like who to marry, where to live and raise a family, and what career path to pursue. These choices can have a profound impact on our lives and legacy.

The good news is that we are not left to our own devices or required to figure life out on our own. God's word provides guidance on practically every issue of life. Psalm 119:105 states that God's word is a lamp to our feet and a light to our path, and in Psalm 32:8, God promises to guide us along the best pathway for our lives.

So, we can ask for and expect God's guidance, but ultimately, the choice is ours to make. We must choose wisely. In Deuteronomy 30:19, God says, "I call heaven and earth as witnesses against you today that I have set before you, life and death, blessing and curse.

Choose life, so that you and your descendants may live." This scripture makes it crystal clear that every choice we make affects not only us, but our children and future generations. It is critical that we choose right.

I heard Joyce Meyer once say: "Every choice you make is a seed you sow, and every seed you sow, brings a harvest in your life of good or bad. Be an investor, not a gambler. An investor makes a decision to do the right thing today, even if he's not yet getting the right result. But a gambler will do the foolish thing, hoping that they'll get by with it and still get a good result."

The point is simple. Our everyday choices matter, because those choices cumulatively determine our future and become our destiny. With every choice, we are writing the story of our lives, and the legacy that we will leave on planet earth. This point is vividly illustrated by the real life accounts in this book. First Corinthians 10:11 tells us that these stories are recorded as examples and warnings for us. We must pay attention to these warning signs on the highway of life so that we do not become spiritual roadkill.

ACKNOWLEDGMENTS

1. Every book is the result of the work of a team, and this book is no exception.
2. Thank you to my friend and partner the Holy Spirit, who is my counselor and guide in daily decision making.
3. Thanks to my children, Emmanuel, Timothy, and Rhema, whose support and love keep me motivated.
4. Thanks to my family and friends for their thoughts, feedback, and encouragement along the way.
5. I am deeply grateful to God my Father, for His call on my life, His grace, and for the privilege of writing this book.
6. This book is a joint effort by many. I am truly grateful for the privilege and partnership. I am better because of you.

NOTES

CHAPTER 1: THE PEOPLE'S MAN

1. The Holy Bible

CHAPTER 2: MIDDLE EAST GREED

1. The Holy Bible

2. J.C Coghlan said, D.D. The Doctrine of Balaam, Bible Hub.

3. I AM The God Kind, Living in the Reality of Your Identity in Christ, Gloria Godson, LifeWork Press, 2021.

4. 10 Surprising Facts About Palm Trees, Anna Norris, Treehugger, April 14, 2021.

5. Who Was Mary Magdalene? Got Questions.org

CHAPTER 3: BEHOLD EL ROI

1. The Holy Bible

2. W.H.O.L.E: 5 Practical Steps to Wholeness in Spirit, Soul, and Body, LifeWork Press, 2022.

CHAPTER 4: THE HIGH COST OF LOW LIVING

1. The Holy Bible

2. Single and Happy, Are You A W.H.O.L.E Single? Xulon Press 2019.

OTHER BOOKS BY THE AUTHOR

1. *W.H.O.L.E:* 5 Practical Steps to Wholeness in Spirit, Soul, and Body, *LifeWork Press, 2022.*

2. *Reclaim Your Destiny,* 31 Day Proclamations to Build Christ Esteem and Godly Self Image, *LifeWork Press, 2022.*

3. The Colt Story, LifeWork Press, 2021.

4. I AM The God Kind, Living in the Reality of Your Identity in Christ, LifeWork Press, 2021.

5. Fight to Win with Prayer and Proclamations, Grivante Press, 2020.

6. Single and Happy, Are You A W.H.O.L.E Single? Xulon Press 2019.

7. Choosing a Life of Victory, Xulon Press 2019.

8. Single and Happy, Are You A W.H.O.L.E Single? Study Guide.

9. Workbook: 5 Practical Steps to Wholeness in Spirit, Soul, and Body.

AUTHOR MINISTRY RESOURCES

LIFEWORK MINISTRIES, INC.
LifeWork Ministries empowers people to live the abundant life in Christ. We preach, write, and witness! Our compelling mission is to release the Life of Christ into the world by using our faith, thinking our faith, speaking our faith, singing our faith, praying our faith and sharing our faith. Connect with us on our website: **www.lifeworkministries.org** or send us an email at **lifeworkministriesinc@gmail.com**

WEEKLY RADIO BROADCAST
Gloria has a weekly Bible teaching radio program. You can hear her radio broadcast in cities across America. For the schedule of her weekly radio bible teaching program or to listen to her radio broadcast, go to our website: **www.lifeworkministries.org.**

LICENSED CLINICAL PASTORAL COUNSELOR & TEMPERAMENT COUNSELOR
At LifeWork Ministries, we provide individual, family, marriage, pre-marital, relationship, career, ministry, and teen counseling. Contact us on our website at **www.lifeworkministries.org**

iDECLARE PRAYER AND PROCLAMATION
Gloria hosts the iDECLARE Prayer and Proclamation event. The word of God, spoken in faith, is the most powerful weapon known to man. At iDECLARE, we load, cock, and fire the word of God to transform our lives, families, and nations!

RACIAL EQUITY & UNITY
Gloria leads the Biblical Equity and Unity (BEU) collaborative, hosts the monthly BEU Community dialogue, and the annual Racial Equity and Unity luncheon. Our vision is to educate, engage, and advocate on issues of biblical equity and unity; and to promote racial reconciliation and healing. We are at: Facebook@REUofDE.

SAVED SINGLES SUMMIT

Gloria hosts the Saved Singles Summit, a premier Christ-centered forum, which brings together Christian singles from churches across America for a time of fun, fellowship, empowerment, kingdom connections and new opportunities. Join us at:
www.savedsinglessummit.com. Facebook@savedsinglessummit.

SINGLE CHRISTIANS CONNECT MEETUP GROUPS

For clean, fun, weekly activities and social events.
https://www.meetup.com/single-christians-connect/
https://www.meetup.com/philadelphia_single_Christians-connect/

SINGLE SENSE CONVERSATIONS

Monthly interactive, Zoom panel discussion on issues that impact Christian singles, every 4th Friday.

THE GRACETALK

Weekly internet talk show hosted by Gloria on Sundays at 6pm:
https://www.facebook.com/TheGraceTalk/live_videos/

ABOUT THE AUTHOR

Gloria Godson is a multi-faceted corporate executive, with an illustrious career in the Energy Industry. She is a visionary, thought and strategy leader, and consummate senior executive. An attorney by training, she rose through several executive leadership positions to become a Vice President in Exelon Corporation, the largest energy company in America.

Today, in response to God's call, Gloria is a Christian leader, Bible teacher, author, prayer minister, and conference speaker. She is a Licensed Clinical Pastoral Counselor, Certified Temperament Counselor and Professional Clinical Member of the National Christian Counselors Association. She is the CEO of LifeWork Ministries, and has a weekly Bible teaching radio program. She hosts Wholeness Workshops, Temperament Workshops, the premier annual Saved Singles Summit, the iDECLARE Prayer and Proclamation event, the Racial Equity and Unity Community Events, and the live *GraceTalk* internet talk show.

Gloria served on the Board of Word of Life (WOL) Christian Center in Newark, Delaware, a full gospel, non-denominational church, for over twelve years. And for over fifteen years, Gloria also served as overseer of the WOL prayer ministries, and is a regular eye witness to God's miraculous answers to prayer. She is a powerful minister of the word of God, with a singular focus on building lives and the kingdom of God. She is a dynamic speaker who connects with both professional and Christian audiences across the country and around the world.

Gloria loves to serve her community! She is on the Board of Faith and Freedom Coalition Mid-Atlantic. Gloria is an online missionary with Global Media Outreach, a dedicated volunteer with the REACH community outreach, the Sunday Breakfast Mission, Urban Promise, Exceptional Care for Children, and more. She loves God passionately and believes in the unstoppable power of Almighty God to do the impossible. She lives in Delaware, United States.

AUTHOR CONTACT

To invite Gloria to speak, send her your prayer request, place a book order, or simply connect, please go to:

www.lifeworkministries.org

www.gloriagodson.com

Facebook@TheGraceTalk

Instagram@TheGraceTalk

YouTube@TheGraceTalk

LifeWork Ministries, Inc.

P. O. Box 56,

Townsend, DE 19734

www.lifeworkministries.org

EMAIL

lifeworkministriesinc@gmail.com

www.ingramcontent.com/pod-product-compliance
Lightning Source LLC
LaVergne TN
LVHW040151080526
838202LV00042B/3112